THE

UNOFFICIAL

TED LASSO

COOKBOOK

THE
UNOFFICIAL
TED LASSO
COOKBOOK

FROM BISCUITS TO BBQ, 50 RECIPES INSPIRED BY TV'S MOST LOVABLE FOOTBALL TEAM

AKI BERRY AND MEG CHANO

HARVEST
An Imprint of WILLIAM MORROW

THE UNOFFICIAL TED LASSO COOKBOOK. Copyright © 2023 by Aki Berry and Meg Chano. All rights reserved. Printed in the United States of America. No part of this book may be used or reproduced in any manner whatsoever without written permission except in the case of brief quotations embodied in critical articles and reviews. For information, address HarperCollins Publishers, 195 Broadway, New York, NY 10007.

HarperCollins books may be purchased for educational, business, or sales promotional use. For information, please email the Special Markets Department at SPsales@harpercollins.com.

FIRST EDITION

Designed by Tai Blanche

Illustrations by Sammy Gorin

Photography by Meg Chano

Library of Congress Cataloging-in-Publication Data has been applied for.

ISBN 978-0-06-332592-0

23 24 25 26 27 LBC 5 4 3 2 1

TO THOSE WHO BELIEVE

CONTENTS

INTRODUCTION

Who knew that a TV show about an optimistic American football coach who takes a job managing a British premier league team would strike a chord with so many people?

Though Ted Lasso knows zilch about British football, what he lacks in knowledge he makes up for with his genuine kindness and empathy. His unbridled charm and exuberance resonate with us all—Ted Lasso gives us the hope to believe. To believe in one another, believe in teamwork, and, most importantly, to believe in ourselves.

This cookbook is a celebration of the spirit and themes found in *Ted Lasso*. Inspired by Ted's world, it features recipes that mirror the scenes and characters from the show: from hearty meals found in bustling pubs to traditional American fare. There are also dishes inspired by different characters and scenes, like Sam Obisanya's jollof rice, or Dani Rojas's Mexican ponche, so this book is as diverse as AFC Richmond itself.

As it turns out, Coach Lasso's sage advice works just as well in the kitchen as it does on a football pitch. Here are the top five Ted Lasso–inspired lessons for cooking:

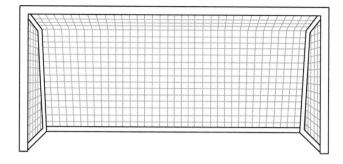

1. A new recipe always smells like potential. Even if it appears daunting, trust the process, and if all else fails, remember: it's still (hopefully) edible.

2. Be a goldfish with a ten-second memory. Sometimes, it's okay to give one recipe a break and try another.

3. Be curious, not judgmental. Sure, some recipes might seem strange to you, but they're perfectly normal elsewhere. Treat each recipe and ingredient with respect because someone, somewhere, loves it.

4. What may taste like a flavorful cup of tea to one person may actually be hot brown water (or absolute garbage water) to another. That's okay, as long as you love it.

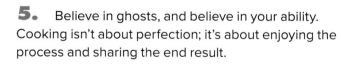

5. Believe in ghosts, and believe in your ability. Cooking isn't about perfection; it's about enjoying the process and sharing the end result.

Have fun exploring the connections between the show and these recipes—falling even more in love with the world and the cast of *Ted Lasso*. Most importantly, remember to believe in yourself and believe in the magic of cooking.

GOLDFISH MIX

Don't be a goldfish and forget to make this for your next gathering. Sassy and playful, this goldfish mix is perfect for snacking. Make a batch to share with teammates, serve as pre–game day snacks, or bring to family potlucks. This mix is tangy and crunchy and loaded with irresistible goldfish, bagel bites, and Chex. Watch these little fishies fly out of the bowl—they're that good.

SERVES 8 TO 10

- ½ cup (1 stick) unsalted butter, melted
- 1 tablespoon hot sauce
- 3 tablespoons Worcestershire sauce
- 1 tablespoon onion powder
- 2 tablespoons packed dark brown sugar
- 2½ teaspoons garlic powder

- 1½ teaspoons ground mustard
- 1½ teaspoons seasoned salt (like Lawry's)
- ½ teaspoon smoked paprika
- 4 cups preferred variety of Chex (or use a mix)
- 2 cups goldfish
- 1½ cups bagel chips
- ½ cup grated Parmesan

1. Set an oven rack in the middle position and preheat the oven to 250°F.

2. In a small bowl, whisk together the melted butter, hot sauce, Worcestershire sauce, onion powder, brown sugar, garlic powder, ground mustard, seasoned salt, and paprika.

3. In a separate larger bowl, toss together the Chex, goldfish, and bagel chips.

4. Pour the melted spice mixture over the dry Chex mixture and stir to coat.

5. Stir in the grated Parmesan and mix well.

6. Transfer to the prepared baking sheet and spread the mixture in an even layer.

7. Bake for 30 minutes. Remove from the oven, give the mixture a good toss, and bake for an additional 30 minutes, or until dry and fragrant. Cool before serving.

8. Store leftovers in an airtight container at room temperature for up to 1 week.

> **EQUIPMENT**
> - **Parchment-lined half baking sheet**

SEASON 1, EPISODE 2

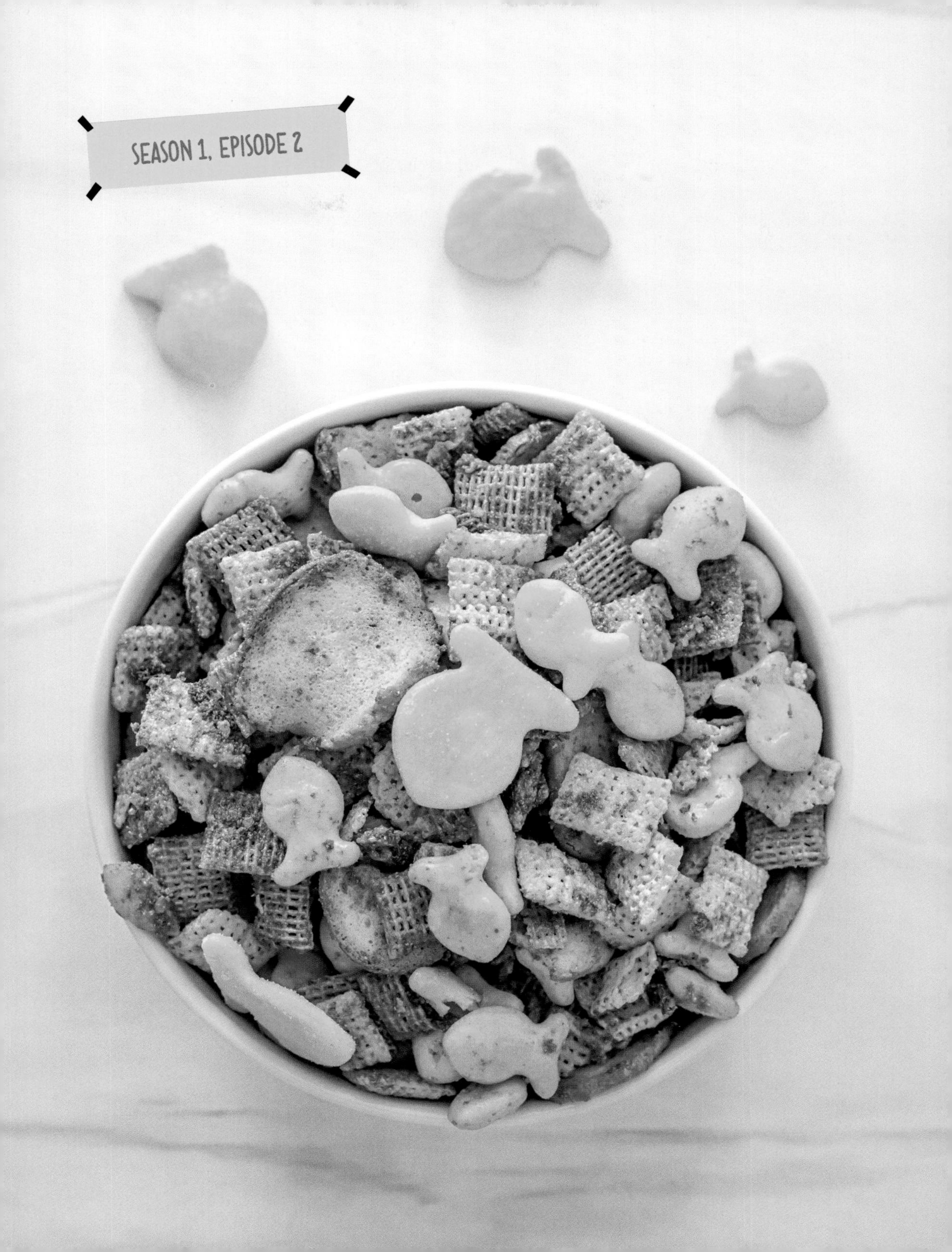

SNEAKY, SALTY BITCH BITES

Sometimes mistakes can have the best outcomes, like when the sugar is swapped for salt. That's how these Sneaky, Salty Bitch Bites first made an appearance. This cheesy coin cracker is bursting with three types of cheese, and truffle salt lends an earthy flavor. Plus, since there's no sugar in this recipe, even Dr. Sharon can indulge in them.

MAKES 30 BITES

- ¾ cup rice flour
- 6 tablespoons unsalted butter, cubed and chilled
- ½ cup shredded sharp white Cheddar
- ½ cup shredded Gruyère
- ¼ cup plus 2 tablespoons grated Parmesan
- ½ teaspoon truffle salt, plus more for dusting
- 1 teaspoon white truffle oil
- ½ teaspoon freshly ground black pepper
- 3 to 5 tablespoons ice water

1. In the food processor, pulse the flour, butter cubes, Cheddar, Gruyère, ¼ cup of the Parmesan, the truffle salt, truffle oil, and pepper until well combined.

2. Add 3 tablespoons of the ice water to the flour mixture and pulse until combined. If needed, add more water in 1-tablespoon increments until the dough comes together.

3. Remove half of the dough and wrap it in plastic wrap. Roll it with your hands to form a rod, about 4 inches long and 1½ inches in diameter. Repeat this with the remaining dough.

4. Remove the plastic wrap and roll the logs in the remaining 2 tablespoons Parmesan so that the cheese coats the outside.

5. Cover the logs with plastic wrap and place in the fridge for at least 2 hours, or up to overnight.

6. When ready to bake, set an oven rack in the middle position and preheat the oven to 350°F.

7. Remove the rolled logs from the fridge and cut into ¼-inch rounds; each log will yield approximately 15 rounds.

8. Space the cheesy rounds 1 inch apart on the prepared baking sheet. Bake for 20 to 22 minutes, until the outside is golden brown.

9. Remove from the oven and dust each baked bite with truffle salt. Store leftovers in an airtight container at room temperature for up to 3 days or in the refrigerator for up to 1 week.

NOTE: As the bites cool, they'll continue to crisp. Remove from the baking sheet after about 10 minutes.

EQUIPMENT

- ■ Food processor
- ■ Plastic wrap
- ■ Parchment-lined half baking sheet

SEASON 2, EPISODE 12

CUCUMBER CREAM CHEESE FINGER SANDWICHES

These adorable mini sandwiches are a staple at afternoon tea. Though they can be made with several different fillings, they must be petite and slender to ensure they can be polished off in a few bites. This recipe features thinly sliced cucumber sandwiched between blankets of tangy cream cheese. Stack several finger sandwiches together, serve with a cup of hot brown water, and you've got a mini afternoon tea for two.

SERVES 2

- 2 ounces cream cheese, at room temperature
- 1 tablespoon sour cream
- ½ teaspoon fresh lemon juice
- ¼ teaspoon salt
- 1 to 2 tablespoons unsalted butter, at room temperature
- 4 slices white bread
- 2 small Persian cucumbers, sliced into ⅛-inch rounds

1. In a small bowl, combine the cream cheese, sour cream, lemon juice, and salt. Mix with a spoon until smooth.

2. Spread the butter on 2 pieces of the bread and spread the cream cheese mixture on the remaining 2 slices.

3. Layer the sliced cucumber on top of the cream cheese mixture and then top with the buttered bread to form a sandwich.

4. Trim off the crusts and cut the sandwiches into tiny shapes. Serve immediately or cover and store in the fridge for up to 24 hours.

SEASON 1, EPISODE 2

CAESAR YOU LATER SALAD

Caesar salad is heralded as the most popular of salads, and this recipe is an instant classic. Crisp romaine lettuce is tossed with garlic croutons, while the dressing features salty anchovies and tangy lemon. This unpretentious salad can be served at all occasions, as a light appetizer or a main meal. For the dressing, use half a can of anchovies and save the rest for topping the salad. Whether or not you're having salad in Higgins's office, this salad will surely get a thumbs-up (and Higgins will definitely come back for seconds and Caesar You Later with this salad!).

SERVES 4 TO 6

Dressing
- **5 anchovies (half a 2-ounce can), drained**
- **1 garlic clove**
- **1 tablespoon fresh lemon juice**
- **½ teaspoon Dijon mustard**
- **¼ cup olive oil**
- **1 egg yolk**
- **1 tablespoon mayonnaise**
- **½ cup grated Parmesan**

Salad
- **1 wedge romaine lettuce, chopped**
- **½ cup croutons**
- **Grated Parmesan, for topping (optional)**
- **Anchovies, drained, for topping (optional)**

1. Make the dressing: Using a mortar and pestle, pound the anchovies and garlic to make a paste. Transfer to a small bowl.

2. Whisk the lemon juice, mustard, and olive oil into the anchovy-garlic paste.

3. Whisk in the egg yolk and mayonnaise.

4. Gently fold in the Parmesan. You can use the dressing immediately or store in an airtight container in the fridge for up to 1 day.

5. Assemble the salad: Place the lettuce in a large bowl. Top with the croutons and, if desired, more Parmesan and the anchovies. Just before serving, toss with the salad dressing.

NOTE: If using a food processor, put all the dressing ingredients into the processor and pulse until combined.

EQUIPMENT
- **Mortar and pestle (or food processor; see Note)**

SHE'S A RAINBOW FRUIT BOARD

This bright and colorful appetizer highlights fresh and seasonal fruits. Create this board with local produce and a variety of cheeses and meats, arranging them in the colors of the rainbow. Dedicated to all the rainbows in the world, this beautiful spread will appeal to all walks of life, from broody punks to peppy directors of communications.

SERVES 8 TO 10

Colorful Food Ideas

Red/Dark Pink
Beets
Cherries
Cherry tomatoes
Dragon fruit
Pomegranates
Prosciutto
Radishes
Raspberries
Red bell peppers
Salami
Strawberries
Watermelon

Orange
Carrots
Cheddar cheese
Kumquats
Mangoes
Orange bell peppers
Oranges
Orange tomatoes
Papaya

Yellow
Golden kiwis
Hummus
Lemons
Pears
Pineapple
Star fruits
Sungold tomatoes
Yellow bell peppers
Yellow peaches

Green
Broccoli
Cucumbers
Edamame beans
Green apples
Green cheese
Green figs
Green grapes
Green pears
Guacamole
Kiwis
Snap peas

Dark Blue/Purple
Beets
Blackberries
Black grapes
Blueberries
Figs
Purple carrots
Purple cauliflower
Purple plums
Purple shiso
Red cabbage
Red hummus

Additional Items
Nuts, crackers, cookies, pita wedges, fruit dip, and chips

NOTE: Feel free to get creative and choose whatever rainbow ingredients are in season.

1. Cut the veggies, fruits, and meats into bite-size pieces and place them on the platter in the order of a rainbow: red/pink, orange, yellow, green, blue/purple.

2. To assemble: Place the larger items on the board first, like the cheese wedges or cut fruit. Next, arrange the smaller condiment bowls around the larger items (but don't fill the condiment bowls yet). Then place color-coordinating fruits on the board, in the general color order of a rainbow. Use toothpicks to help prop up and stabilize the fruit if necessary. Once

the large pieces have been placed, you can start filling the platter with smaller items. Save the smallest items like blueberries, nuts, and tiny cubed cheeses for the end to use as filler. Finally, fill the condiment bowls with hummus and fruit dip, and enjoy!

EQUIPMENT

- **Large platter**
- **Assortment of pinch bowls, for condiments**
- **Toothpicks, for stabilizing and arranging fruit**

SEASON 1, EPISODE 6

PIGS IN ROY'S BLANKIE

These tiny hot dogs are wrapped in buttery puff pastry dough, and just like Roy, they are impossible to resist. You can simply buy miniature cocktail doggies and premade puff pastry dough to make this recipe easy-peasy! Roy might have brought a blankie to the break-the-curse ceremony, but you'll be the star of the show when you bring this popular appetizer.

MAKES 30 PIECES

Pigs in a Blankie
- **All-purpose flour, for dusting**
- **1 sheet puff pastry, defrosted**
- **30 cocktail franks (14-ounce package)**
- **1 egg plus 1 tablespoon water, beaten**
- **2 tablespoons poppy seeds or sesame seeds (optional)**

Mustard Dipping Sauce
- **2 tablespoons Dijon mustard**
- **2 tablespoons mayonnaise**
- **1 tablespoon honey**
- **1 teaspoon fresh lemon juice**
- **Pinch of salt**

1. Make the pigs in a blankie: Set an oven rack in the middle position and preheat the oven to 400°F.

2. Dust a clean work surface with flour. Unroll the sheet of puff pastry into a 10 × 10-inch square.

3. Cut the square into 3 equal rectangles, each about 3⅓ inches in width.

4. Divide each rectangle into 10 tiny strips, each about 1 × 3⅓ inches. There should be 30 small strips once finished. Wrap each cocktail frank with 1 strip of puff pastry and place them on the prepared baking sheet.

5. Brush each puff pastry with the egg mixture and then sprinkle the top with seeds.

6. Bake for 22 to 24 minutes, until the crust is golden brown.

7. Remove from the oven and let cool for 10 minutes.

8. Make the dipping sauce: Mix together the sauce ingredients in a small bowl. Serve immediately alongside the pigs in a blankie or chill until ready to use.

9. Store leftover pigs in a blankie in an airtight container in the fridge for up to 4 days. The dipping sauce will keep in an airtight container in the fridge for up to 1 week.

> **EQUIPMENT**
> - **Rolling pin**
> - **Parchment-lined half baking sheet**
> - **Pastry brush**

SEASON 1, EPISODE 10

OLIVE BRANCH SAVORY SCONES

Let's be real, sometimes you'll need to extend an olive branch—for example, when you've been feuding with a teammate for too long on your football team. These savory olive scones are filled with two types of cheeses and loads of black olives, and they're so flavorful that even Roy could share them with Jamie as a way to find common ground.

MAKES 8 SCONES

- 2 cups all-purpose flour, plus more for dusting
- 1 tablespoon baking powder
- 2 tablespoons sugar
- 1 teaspoon ground cumin
- 1¼ teaspoons ground coriander
- 1 teaspoon onion powder
- 1 teaspoon salt
- 6 tablespoons unsalted butter, cubed and chilled
- 1 (2.5-ounce) can black olives, drained
- 1 cup shredded Cheddar
- 1 cup shredded Monterey Jack
- ⅓ cup chopped green onions
- 4 ounces ham steak, cubed
- ⅓ cup heavy cream
- 1 (4-ounce) can hatch chiles, with liquid
- 2 eggs, at room temperature

1. Set an oven rack in the middle position and preheat the oven to 400°F.

2. In a large bowl, mix together the flour, baking powder, sugar, cumin, coriander, onion powder, and salt.

3. Using your fingers or a pastry cutter, mix the butter into the flour mixture until it forms pea-size clumps and resembles coarse wet sand.

4. Gently mix in the olives, cheeses, green onions, and ham and toss to coat.

5. In a medium bowl, mix together the heavy cream, hatch chiles with their liquid, and eggs.

6. Add the wet mixture to the flour mixture and knead together until combined. The dough will be very shaggy.

7. Dust a work surface with flour and turn out the dough. Shape the dough into a 7 × 8-inch rectangle loaf.

8. Cut the rectangle into 8 triangular pieces. With the spatula, transfer the wedges to the prepared baking sheet.

9. Bake for 20 minutes, or until the tops of the scones are golden. Remove and let cool before serving. Store leftovers in an airtight container in the fridge for up to 4 days.

EQUIPMENT
- Pastry cutter (optional)
- Parchment-lined half baking sheet

SAM'S OVEN-BAKED RATATOUILLE

If Sam cooked Rebecca dinner, it would be inspired by his favorite movie, *Ratatouille*. Here, colorful veggies are assembled in a large baking dish with a rich and robust tomato sauce, which is then topped with cheese before baking. Find zucchini, squash, eggplant, tomatoes, and potatoes that are similar in diameter; this way, the rounds will look more uniform when arranged on the platter. It's not just textual chemistry—it's Team Sam for the win!

SERVES 4

- 1 medium red bell pepper, cored, seeded, and quartered
- 1 (14- to 15-ounce) can whole tomatoes
- 2 tablespoons olive oil
- 2 medium shallots, finely chopped
- 2 garlic cloves, finely chopped
- ¼ teaspoon plus a pinch of salt
- ⅛ teaspoon freshly ground black pepper
- ¼ teaspoon smoked paprika
- 1 medium zucchini, sliced into ⅛-inch rounds
- 1 medium yellow squash, sliced into ⅛-inch rounds
- 1 medium Italian or Japanese eggplant, sliced into ⅛-inch rounds
- 3 medium tomatoes, sliced into ⅛-inch rounds
- 2 medium gold potatoes, peeled and sliced into ⅛-inch rounds
- 1 cup shredded Gruyère
- ½ cup shredded or grated Parmesan
- Chopped fresh parsley (optional)

1. Set an oven rack in the top position and preheat the oven to 390°F. In a blender, place the red bell pepper and canned tomatoes and puree until smooth. Set aside.

2. In a skillet, heat 1 tablespoon of the olive oil over medium-high heat.

3. Sauté the shallots and garlic with the pinch of salt for about 3 minutes, until translucent.

4. Add the pureed tomato mixture and cook for about 10 minutes over medium heat, until the sauce thickens.

5. Mix the remaining ¼ teaspoon salt, the black pepper, and smoked paprika into the tomato mixture.

6. Spread the tomato mixture on the bottom of the skillet evenly.

7. Arrange the sliced veggies in a circular pattern in this order: zucchini, yellow squash, eggplant, tomato, and potato, and repeat around the dish. Spread out the veggies so that one round is slightly stacked on another round until all the rounds have been used.

8. Sprinkle the Gruyère and Parmesan on top and drizzle over the remaining 1 tablespoon olive oil.

9. Cover the skillet with aluminum foil. Poke a few holes in the foil so steam can be released.

10. Bake for 30 minutes and then remove the foil and continue baking for an additional 30 minutes. If the top starts to brown too much, re-cover the dish with the foil. Remove the skillet from the oven and let it cool for 10 minutes before serving.

11. Garnish with parsley, if desired, and serve. Store leftovers in an airtight container in the fridge for up to 4 days.

EQUIPMENT

- **Mandoline slicer with a blade of ⅛-inch thickness (optional)**
- **Stand blender**
- **12-inch oven-safe skillet or 9 × 13-inch baking dish**

RICHARD'S FANCY STINKY CHEESE BOARD WITH FAUX GRAS

This stinky cheese board is easy to assemble and a fun way to sample different varieties of cheese. Arrange the cheese on a platter and pick a selection that has a common theme. Some themes can be based on similar geographical locations (French cheese, British cheese), colors (yellow and blue), or textures and smell (soft, hard, mellow, or stinky). Pair this board with Champagne and faux foie gras. While Richard Montlaur brought traditional foie gras to the Higginses' Christmas party, this recipe is for faux gras—a vegetarian version infused with mushrooms and truffles. While no supermodel is included in this board, the platter still might bring you a bit of luck.

SERVES 6 TO 8

Cheese Ideas

Stinky Cheese Types
Époisses
Vieux-Boulogne
Camembert
Limburger

Yellow Cheese Types
Baby Swiss
Cheddar
Colby
Monterey Jack

Blue Cheese Types
Dunbarton
Gorgonzola
Stilton
Wisconsin Cheddar blue

Soft Cheese Types
Brie
Chèvre
Feta

Accompaniments
- Baguette slices
- Breadsticks
- Crackers
- Faux Gras (recipe follows)
- Honey
- Nuts
- Olives
- Pita chips
- Preserves
- Salami
- Sneaky, Salty Bitch Bites (page 4)

In true Richard fashion, the cheese board assembly is simple: Unwrap the cheese. Group the cheeses together by similar characteristics, and fill the board with accompaniments. Use pinch bowls to contain the smaller items like olives and nuts. Enjoy with faux supermodels.

EQUIPMENT
- Large platter, for serving
- Cheese accessories, for serving

[recipe continues]

SEASON 2, EPISODE 4

FAUX GRAS

- 1 cup raw cashews
- 2 tablespoons olive oil
- 1 shallot, roughly chopped
- Pinch of salt
- 2 garlic cloves, roughly chopped
- 8 ounces white mushrooms, roughly chopped

- 2 tablespoons Sauternes or other sweet wine
- 2 tablespoons miso paste
- 2 tablespoons truffle oil
- ½ teaspoon truffle salt
- ¼ teaspoon freshly ground black pepper
- 2 to 3 tablespoons ghee or unsalted butter, for topping

1. Soak the cashews in a small bowl overnight or, for a quick soak, pour boiling water over the cashews and soak for 3 hours. Drain and rinse the cashews. Set aside.

2. In a large skillet, heat the olive oil over medium heat and sauté the shallot with a pinch of salt for about 3 minutes, until translucent.

3. Add the garlic to the skillet and cook until fragrant, 1 to 2 minutes.

4. Increase the heat to medium-high and add the mushrooms. Cook, stirring, until they release their liquid and are cooked through, about 5 minutes.

5. Add the Sauternes and cook for 1 minute. Remove from the heat and let cool.

6. Transfer the cooked ingredients to the bowl of a food processor. Add the cashews, miso, truffle oil, truffle salt, and pepper and pulse until smooth.

7. Transfer the cashew mixture to the jar or ramekin and smooth it down so that this first layer is flat.

8. Melt the ghee in a small microwave-safe bowl or in a small saucepan on the stove over low heat. Pour over the cashew mixture. The ghee layer should be ⅛ to ¼ inch thick.

9. Refrigerate for a few hours to set the ghee. Add to the cheese board and enjoy with baguette slices or crackers. Store leftovers in an airtight container in the fridge for up to 5 days.

> **EQUIPMENT**
> - Food processor
> - 2 (8-ounce) jars or ramekins

JACKET POTATOES

The Brits take their pub fare seriously, and these jacket potatoes are no exception. Ridiculously simple, they're creamy and decadent with a brilliantly crisp skin. They are best served straight from the oven, topped with a generous dollop of butter and a sprinkle of salt and pepper. Or, if you prefer, dress them up with green onions, bacon bits, and cheese.

SERVES 4

- 4 russet potatoes, unpeeled, scrubbed and dried

For Serving (optional)
- Salted butter
- Pinch of salt
- Freshly ground black pepper
- Green onions
- Bacon bits
- Grated cheese

1. Set an oven rack in the top position and preheat the oven to 400°F.

2. Cut a ¼-inch-deep cross into the top of each potato. The cross should run almost but not quite the full length of the potato.

3. Place the potatoes on the wire rack on the baking sheet and bake for 1 hour and 45 minutes, or until the potato skin gets crispy and lightly brown / toasted.

4. Using tongs, carefully remove the potatoes from the oven and recut the cross 1 to 2 inches deeper. Return the potatoes to the oven and bake for an additional 15 minutes.

5. Place the hot potatoes on a stable surface. Using a towel or spoon to protect your hands from the heat, squeeze together the two shorter sides of the skin to pop up the potato innards.

6. Top with heaps of butter and season with salt and pepper. Serve hot with any other topping of your choosing. Store leftovers loosely covered in the fridge for up to 4 days.

EQUIPMENT
- Sharp paring knife or other small blade
- Half baking sheet with oven-safe wire rack
- Kitchen tongs or kitchen gloves

CHEESY CORN

Ted might not be in Kansas anymore, but cheesy corn is a midwestern staple that's simple enough to make abroad. Ham and crumbled bacon bits make this dish a satisfying side. You'll need a heavy wooden spoon to mix these ingredients.

SERVES 8 TO 10

- 2 tablespoons unsalted butter, plus more for greasing
- 4 slices bacon
- 1 cup whole milk
- ¼ teaspoon paprika
- ¼ teaspoon garlic powder
- ¼ teaspoon salt
- 3 tablespoons all-purpose flour
- 1 (8-ounce) package cream cheese, cubed and at room temperature
- 1 cup shredded medium Cheddar
- 1 cup shredded pepper Jack
- 1 (16-ounce) bag frozen roasted corn, thawed
- 8 ounces ham steak, chopped into tiny cubes
- Chopped fresh parsley (optional)

1. Set an oven rack in the middle position and preheat the oven to 350°F.

2. Grease the baking dish with butter. Set aside.

3. Fry the bacon in a large pan over medium heat until crispy. Remove the bacon to a plate lined with paper towels. Reserve 2 tablespoons of the bacon fat in the pan. Once the bacon is cool, crumble and set aside.

4. Mix together the milk, paprika, garlic powder, and salt in a small bowl.

5. Melt the butter with the reserved bacon fat. Sprinkle in the flour and stir constantly over medium heat to make a roux, 3 to 5 minutes. No streaks of flour should be visible.

6. Slowly pour the milk mixture into the flour, stirring vigorously. The gravy will thicken as it cooks.

7. Once thickened, add the cream cheese and stir with the heavy wooden spoon. Add the shredded Cheddar and pepper Jack and stir until combined.

8. Once all the cheese has melted, toss in the crumbled bacon bits, corn, and ham. Give the mixture a good stir.

9. Pour the corn mixture into the prepared baking dish.

10. Bake for 30 minutes. Adjust the heat to broil and broil for 1 to 2 minutes, until the top is bubbly and brown. Remove and let cool for 15 minutes before serving. Store leftovers in an airtight container in the fridge for up to 4 days.

EQUIPMENT
- Heavy wooden spoon
- 9 × 13-inch baking dish

GENTLEMAN'S RELISH BRUSCHETTA
WITH BURRATA

Don't let this formal name fool you. Gentleman's relish, a glorified anchovy butter, is a nineteenth-century British savory. Eaten in gentlemen's clubs and reserved for highbrow society, it's a salty marriage of anchovies, herbs, and butter. In this recipe, briny anchovy is mellowed out with creamy burrata cheese and given an extra depth of flavor with prosciutto and peppery arugula. Definitely be curious, not judgmental, when trying this salty relish.

MAKES 6 BRUSCHETTA SLICES

Gentleman's Relish
- ½ teaspoon fresh thyme
- 2 teaspoons capers, drained
- 1 garlic clove
- 1 (2-ounce) can anchovies, drained
- 1 teaspoon fresh lemon juice
- Pinch of ground cinnamon (optional)
- 3 tablespoons unsalted butter, at room temperature

Bruschetta
- 1 baguette, sliced into six ¼-inch rounds and toasted
- ½ cup baby arugula
- 2 slices prosciutto, cut into 6 small pieces
- 1 burrata ball, broken up into small pieces
- Freshly ground black pepper

1. Make the relish: Using a mortar and pestle, pound the thyme until it turns to paste. Add the capers and garlic and continue to pound. Add the anchovies and pound until all of the ingredients are integrated.

2. Transfer from the mortar to a larger bowl if necessary. Stir in the lemon juice, cinnamon (if using), and butter until the paste is uniformly smooth.

3. Assemble the bruschetta: Spread a thin layer of relish onto a toast slice.

4. Top with a few pieces of arugula and prosciutto and a piece of burrata. Season with pepper.

5. Repeat the steps for the remaining 5 slices of toast.

6. Store leftover relish in an airtight container in the fridge for up to 5 days.

NOTE: If using a food processor, simply add all the ingredients except the butter and pulse to combine. Transfer into a small ramekin and fold in the butter.

EQUIPMENT
- Mortar and pestle (or food processor; see Note)

SOUTHERN SLAW

Coleslaw is a side that is found at most southern parties and gatherings. It's a dish that's as ubiquitous to American BBQ as mushy peas are to British fish and chips. This slaw has a sweet and tangy crunch with tons of color, and it's a great choice to balance out heavier meals. Be sure to shred the vegetables as thin as possible so the slaw has a light texture. You can adjust the apple cider vinegar to taste. Make a batch to serve with your favorite American and British meals.

SERVES 4 TO 6

- ½ medium green cabbage, cored and finely shredded
- ¼ small red cabbage, cored and finely shredded
- 1 large carrot, shredded
- ¼ cup mayonnaise
- ¼ cup sour cream
- 1½ teaspoons apple cider vinegar
- 2 teaspoons sugar
- ½ teaspoon salt
- ½ teaspoon caraway seeds

1. Combine the cabbages and carrots in a large bowl.

2. In a small bowl, mix together the mayonnaise, sour cream, vinegar, sugar, salt, and caraway seeds.

3. Pour the dressing over the cabbage and toss to combine. Chill before serving.

4. Store leftovers in an airtight container in the fridge for up to 2 days.

EQUIPMENT
- **Mandoline, for shredding (optional)**

TED'S BULL'S-EYE BBQ PULLED PORK SANDWICH

BBQ is a traditional American meal, and there are many cities that lay claim to the best BBQ. Though American-style BBQ is traditionally smoked, this BBQ recipe doesn't call for complicated smoking tools; instead, it's made in a Dutch oven and baked for a long time with low heat. The resulting pulled pork is moist, tender, and tangy. It's great as a stand-alone meal or used for sandwiches, and it's versatile enough to be paired with different sides. You'll hit a bull's-eye with this awesome recipe, but whatever you do, remember this: it's all about the BBQ sauce.

SERVES 6 TO 8, PLUS MORE FOR LEFTOVERS

Pulled Pork
- 1 tablespoon ground white pepper
- 2 tablespoons chili powder
- 2 tablespoons ground cumin
- 2 tablespoons packed dark brown sugar
- 2 tablespoons dried oregano
- 3 tablespoons smoked paprika
- 1 tablespoon salt
- 1 teaspoon ground mustard
- 2 teaspoons ground coriander
- 2 teaspoons onion powder
- 2 teaspoons garlic powder

- 4 to 5 pounds boneless Boston butt or pork shoulder, cut into 3 × 3-inch cubes
- High-smoke-point oil, such as canola or avocado
- 1 medium white onion, roughly chopped
- 1½ cups ale
- 2 tablespoons Worcestershire sauce
- ¼ cup apple cider vinegar
- 1½ cups beef broth

For Serving
- Burger buns
- BBQ Sauce (recipe follows)
- Southern Slaw (page 30; optional)

1. Set an oven rack in the middle position and preheat the oven to 300°F.

2. Make the pulled pork: Combine the white pepper, chili powder, cumin, brown sugar, oregano, smoked paprika, salt, ground mustard, coriander, and onion and garlic powders to make the dry rub.

3. Massage the rub over the pork cubes, making sure to coat it evenly on all sides. Save any extra dry rub for later.

4. Heat 1 tablespoon oil in the Dutch oven over high heat and brown the pork in small batches. Once the pork has browned on all sides, remove with the tongs and set aside before adding more pork to brown. Continue until all the pork has been browned, adding more oil as necessary.

5. Reduce the heat to medium-high. Add 1 tablespoon oil to the Dutch oven and sauté the onion until soft, about 5 minutes.

[*recipe continues*]

SEASON 1, EPISODE 2
SEASON 1, EPISODE 8

6. Deglaze the pan by adding the ale, Worcestershire sauce, vinegar, and broth. Bring the liquid to a boil, then turn off the heat. Carefully add the pork with the tongs and any extra dry rub to the hot liquid and stir to ensure the pork and dry rub are well mixed in.

7. Cover the Dutch oven and place in the oven for 3 hours.

8. Remove the lid and cook for an additional hour, or until the pork is fork tender, easy to shred, and falls apart easily.

9. Drain the excess liquid and shred the pork.

10. To assemble the sandwiches, top the buns with the pulled pork, BBQ sauce, and, if desired, slaw. Store leftover pork in an airtight container in the fridge for up to 4 days.

NOTE: Alternative pressure cooker method: If there's no available Dutch oven, or if you're short on time, cooking the pork in a pressure cooker gets equally amazing results. To do this, follow steps 1 to 6 using the sauté function. Then pressure cook on high for 40 minutes, followed by natural release for 10 minutes and then quick release. Finish by draining any excess liquid and shredding the pork.

EQUIPMENT

- **5- to 6-quart Dutch oven or oven-safe heavy pot with a tight-fitting lid (or pressure cooker; see Note)**
- **Tongs**

BBQ SAUCE

MAKES 1½ CUPS

- **1½ cups ketchup**
- **2 tablespoons apple cider vinegar**
- **2 tablespoons packed dark brown sugar**
- **1 teaspoon ground mustard**
- **1 teaspoon onion powder**
- **½ teaspoon garlic powder**
- **¼ cup ale**
- **⅛ teaspoon salt**

1. In a small saucepan, mix the BBQ sauce ingredients together and bring to a boil over high heat.

2. Reduce the heat slightly to bring the sauce to a slow boil (the edges will bubble). Cook for 5 minutes. Lower the heat to medium-low and cover. Cook for an additional 10 minutes, or until the sauce has thickened, stirring occasionally. Remove from the heat and set aside until ready to use. Store leftovers in an airtight container in the fridge for up to 1 week.

MUM'S SHEPHERD'S PIE
WITH CHEESY TOP

Commonly found in British pubs, traditional shepherd's pie is made with ground lamb and veggies and then topped with a creamy mashed potato crust. Inspired by Rebecca's favorite childhood recipe, this version incorporates Cheddar cheese into the potatoes. This recipe is flexible, so you can substitute whatever is on hand for the meat, veggies, and potatoes. Mum's Shepherd's Pie with Cheesy Top also contains white wine for a more sophisticated, grown-up edge Rebecca would be sure to appreciate.

SERVES 6 TO 8

Mum's Shepherd's Pie Filling
- 1 tablespoon oil
- 1 pound ground lamb
- 1 small white onion, roughly chopped
- 1 teaspoon dried thyme
- 2 garlic cloves, minced
- 2½ cups frozen vegetable medley of peas, carrots, green beans, and corn
- 1 teaspoon Worcestershire sauce
- 2 tablespoons tomato paste
- ¼ cup dry white wine
- 1 teaspoon salt

- 1 tablespoon plus 1 teaspoon all-purpose flour
- 1 cup beef broth

Mash Topping
- 2 pounds potatoes, peeled and cut into 1-inch rounds (see Notes)
- 3 tablespoons unsalted butter
- ⅓ cup heavy cream, plus more if needed
- ½ teaspoon salt
- 2 cups shredded medium Cheddar
- 2 egg yolks
- Chopped fresh parsley (optional)

1. Make the shepherd's pie: In a large sauté pan, heat the oil over medium-high heat. Add the lamb and brown, breaking it up with a wooden spoon, 6 to 8 minutes. With a slotted spoon, transfer the lamb to a plate lined with paper towels and set aside.

2. Add the onion to the pan and sauté in the leftover oil until translucent, about 5 minutes.

3. Add the thyme and minced garlic. Cook until fragrant, 1 to 2 minutes.

4. Add the frozen vegetables and cook until thawed, about 3 minutes.

5. Return the cooked lamb to the veggie mixture and mix in.

6. Add the Worcestershire sauce, tomato paste, wine, and salt. Cook for

[*recipe continues*]

SEASON 2, EPISODE 6

2 minutes, stirring to incorporate all the ingredients.

7. Add the flour and cook for a few minutes, stirring, until no streaks of flour are visible.

8. Gradually add the broth and let simmer. Keep stirring the mixture until the liquid has a gravy-like consistency, about 5 minutes.

9. Make the mash topping: Place the potatoes in a large pot, cover with water, and bring to a boil over high heat. Cook until tender, 13 to 15 minutes.

10. Drain the water, then add the butter, heavy cream, and salt to the pot with the potatoes. Mash until smooth.

11. Once slightly cooled, add the cheese to the mixture and continue to mash.

12. Wait for the potatoes to cool even more before adding the yolks (if the potatoes are too hot, the eggs will scramble). Mix the yolks in with the mash.

13. Assemble the pie: Set an oven rack in the middle position and preheat the oven to 375°F.

14. Spread the lamb mixture evenly in the bottom of the baking dish.

15. With an offset spatula or the back of a spoon, spread the mashed potatoes on top of the lamb. If you want fancy swirls on the mash, use a fork to sketch out a pattern before baking.

16. Bake for 25 minutes, or until bubbly and the top is browned.

17. Let sit for 15 minutes. Garnish with parsley and serve. Store leftovers in an airtight container in the fridge for up to 4 days.

NOTE: You can use whichever potatoes you have on hand, but Yukon gold potatoes will result in a creamier mashed potato, while russet potatoes will yield a fluffier mash.

EQUIPMENT
- **Slotted spoon**
- **9 × 13-inch baking dish (3 quarts) or 6 single serving baking dishes (0.5 quart**

CHICKEN TIKKA MASALA WITH RICE

While we don't know what Ollie's father-in-law recommended for Trent Crimm and Ted when they met for a meal at his restaurant, we suspect it could be the popular Indian dish chicken tikka masala. This dish is so iconic in the UK that it's often considered to be the national dish of England, though there is some debate as to where it actually originated. Making tikka masala is a labor of love, but it's worth the time and commitment for this rich and satisfying dish. If you're okay with a little bit of spice, then keep the measurements the same as the recipe instructs; otherwise, for a milder flavor—if you want your tongue still in your mouth and your intestinal system intact—adjust or omit the hot chili powder. Dig in!

NOTE: We've also included a bonus recipe for Ollie's father-in-law's curry powder, which can be used in any recipe calling for curry powder.

Kashmiri chili powder is mild and is used to brighten up the appearance of curry and chicken marinade.

SERVES 6 TO 8

Chicken Marinade
- **1 cup plain whole milk yogurt**
- **4 garlic cloves, minced**
- **1 tablespoon minced peeled fresh ginger**
- **1 tablespoon neutral oil**
- **1 teaspoon fresh lemon juice**
- **1 tablespoon paprika**
- **2 tablespoons Ollie's Father-in-Law's Curry Powder (recipe follows; see Notes) or store-bought curry powder**
- **1 teaspoon salt**
- **1 teaspoon Kashmiri chili powder (see Notes)**
- **2 pounds skinless, boneless chicken thighs, patted dry and cut into 1-inch cubes**

Curry Sauce
- **4 tablespoons butter or ghee**
- **1 large red or yellow onion, finely chopped**
- **4 garlic cloves, minced**
- **1 tablespoon minced peeled fresh ginger**
- **2 tablespoons Ollie's Father-in-Law's Curry Powder (recipe follows) or store-bought curry powder**
- **2 teaspoons garam masala**
- **1 tablespoon tomato paste**
- **1 (14- to 15-ounce) can tomato sauce**
- **1 teaspoon Kashmiri chili powder**
- **1 to 2 teaspoons hot chili powder (optional for hotter taste)**
- **1 teaspoon paprika**
- **1 teaspoon salt**
- **1 cup heavy cream**
- **1½ teaspoons honey**
- **Chopped fresh cilantro (optional)**

For serving
- **Basmati Rice (recipe follows)**
- **Naan (optional)**

[*recipe continues*]

1. Make the chicken marinade: In a large bowl, mix together the yogurt, garlic, ginger, oil, lemon juice, paprika, curry powder, salt, and Kashmiri chili powder.

2. Add the chicken cubes, coat well, and marinate in the fridge overnight if possible, but if you're in a time crunch, for at least 1 hour.

3. Set an oven rack in the top position and preheat the oven to 450°F. Remove the chicken from the marinade and place on the prepared baking sheet.

4. Bake the chicken for 20 minutes, or until lightly browned. The chicken will continue to cook in the curry in a later step.

5. Make the curry sauce: In a large pot, melt the butter over medium heat.

6. Sauté the onion until translucent, 4 to 5 minutes.

7. Add garlic and ginger and sauté until fragrant, 1 to 2 minutes.

8. Add the curry powder, garam masala, and tomato paste, stirring to incorporate. Add the tomato sauce, Kashmiri chili powder, hot chili powder (if using), paprika, and salt and mix well.

9. Add the chicken and ¼ cup water to the pot, stir, and cover. Cook for 15 to 20 minutes, removing the lid to stir occasionally.

10. Reduce the heat to low and add the heavy cream and honey. Simmer for an additional 5 to 10 minutes, uncovered, stirring occasionally. Garnish with cilantro (if using) and serve with rice and, if desired, naan. Store leftovers in an airtight container in the fridge for up to 4 days or in the freezer for up to 1 month.

EQUIPMENT
- **Parchment-lined half baking sheet**

SEASON 1, EPISODE 3

OLLIE'S FATHER-IN-LAW'S CURRY POWDER

MAKES ABOUT ⅓ CUP

- 2 tablespoons ground coriander
- 2 tablespoons ground cumin
- 1 tablespoon ground cayenne pepper
- 1½ teaspoons ground turmeric
- ½ teaspoon freshly ground black pepper
- ½ teaspoon ground cardamom
- 1 teaspoon ground ginger
- ¼ teaspoon ground cloves
- ¼ teaspoon ground nutmeg
- ¼ teaspoon ground cinnamon

In a small bowl, combine all the ingredients. Store leftover curry powder in an airtight container at room temperature for up to 6 months.

NOTES: Homemade curry powder has a robust flavor and a long shelf life. If you need another recipe to use it in, try Sam's Jollof Rice with Chicken (page 51).

BASMATI RICE

- **2 cups basmati rice**

1. Rinse the rice and drain well. Repeat several times, until the water runs clear.

2. Place the rice and 2½ cups of water in a medium pot, cover, and bring to a boil over high heat. Immediately reduce the heat to low and simmer, covered, for 7 to 10 minutes, until all the water evaporates.

3. Turn off the heat and allow the rice to steam, still covered, for an additional 5 minutes. Once ready to serve, give the rice a good stir, incorporating the rice from the bottom to the top. Serve with tikka masala.

NOTE: Alternative pressure cooker method: Pressure cook the rice in the water on low for 3 minutes, followed by natural release for 5 minutes and then quick release.

NATE THE GREAT'S HOT DOG, THREE WAYS

Hot dogs are an American pastime, and different American cities each boast their own style of dog as the best. For an around-the-states hot dog tour, here are some fun ways to plate up a few regional varieties: Create a Chicago dog by loading up on the dill pickles, jalapeños, pepperoncini, onions, tomatoes, and mustard. For a West Coast Seattle dog, spread cream cheese on the bun, and then pile on onions and fresh jalapeños. And for a Kansas City dog, toss on some sauerkraut, pulled pork, and melted Swiss cheese. Whip up a few versions and let people pick their own toppings. They may not have Nathan's hot dogs in the UK, but with this recipe, you can still enjoy this American pastime. Place them on a large platter that's perfect for a tailgate . . . with Nate the Great!

MAKES 3 HOT DOGS

- 3 all-beef Nathan's Famous hot dogs
- 3 hot dog buns

Toppings for 1 Seattle dog
- 1 tablespoon unsalted butter
- ¼ medium white onion, thinly sliced
- Pinch of salt
- 1 ounce cream cheese, at room temperature
- 1 jalapeño, thinly sliced

Toppings for 1 Chicago dog
- 1 dill pickle spear
- 1 jalapeño, thinly sliced
- 2 pepperoncini, thinly sliced
- 2 tablespoons diced white onion
- 2 tablespoons diced tomato
- 1 tablespoon yellow mustard
- Poppy seeds (optional)

Toppings for 1 Kansas City dog
- 2 tablespoons sauerkraut
- ¼ cup pulled pork (see page 34)
- 2 tablespoons shredded Swiss

1. Cook the hot dogs according to your preferred method (boil, panfry, or grill) and set aside.

2. Make the Seattle dog: In a small skillet, melt the butter over medium heat and sauté the onion with a pinch of salt until slightly softened and browned, about 10 minutes. Set aside.

3. Spread the cream cheese on one side of the bun. Pop the hot dog in the middle of the bun and then top with jalapeños and caramelized onions.

4. Make the Chicago dog: Place the hot dog in the bun. Arrange a dill pickle spear, jalapeños, pepperoncini, onion, and tomato on top of the hot dog. Top with mustard and, if desired, sprinkle with poppy seeds.

5. Make the Kansas City dog: Place the hot dog in the bun. Top with the sauerkraut, pulled pork, and shredded Swiss.

6. Pop under the broiler for 1 to 2 minutes, until the cheese is melted.

CHICKEN CORDON BLEU

Looking for a dinner idea that's sure to impress your new love interest? In this fancy dish, chicken, cheese, and prosciutto unite in a scrumptious roll and then are panfried and baked, for a deliciously golden, crisp crust with a melted cheesy center. Keeley will find chicken cordon bleu more romantic than a coffee date, and remember, Nigella says if you butterfly the chicken, it will be more moist.

SERVES 4

Chicken Cordon Bleu

- **4 skinless, boneless chicken breast halves**
- **Salt and freshly ground black pepper**
- **4 thin slices prosciutto or ham**
- **4 slices Swiss or Gruyère**
- **¼ cup all-purpose flour**
- **1 egg, beaten**
- **1 cup panko or other bread crumbs**
- **¼ cup high-smoke-point oil, such as canola or avocado**
- **Chopped fresh parsley (optional)**

Dijon Cream Sauce

- **2 tablespoons unsalted butter**
- **2 tablespoons all-purpose flour**
- **1½ cups whole milk**
- **3 tablespoons Dijon mustard**
- **¼ cup grated Parmesan**
- **1 teaspoon chicken bouillon paste or ⅓ chicken bouillon cube**
- **Pinch of salt**

1. Make the chicken cordon bleu: Set an oven rack in the middle position and preheat the oven to 350°F.

2. Pat the chicken dry with paper towels.

3. Butterfly the chicken: Holding a knife parallel to a cutting board, cut horizontally through the breast, starting at the thickest part and ending at the thinner part. Be careful not to cut all the way through the breast.

4. Open the chicken breasts like a book and place the chicken between two sheets of parchment paper. Pound the chicken with a rolling pin until the thickness is ¼ inch throughout. Repeat this for the other breasts.

5. Sprinkle salt and pepper on both sides of the breasts.

6. Layer the sliced prosciutto and cheese on top of the chicken so the bottom edge of the cheese is aligned with the bottom edge of the chicken.

7. Roll the stack tightly together and secure with a toothpick. Repeat this for the other butterflied chicken breasts.

[recipe continues]

8. Prepare the three dredging bowls. Put the flour in one bowl, the beaten egg in another, and the panko in the third bowl.

9. Dip a chicken breast in the flour mixture. Shake off the excess flour and then dredge the chicken in the egg mixture. Last, roll it in the panko. Repeat for the remaining chicken breasts.

10. Heat the oil in a large frying pan over medium-high heat. Working in two batches, add the breaded chicken and pan-fry until the crust gets golden, 2 to 3 minutes per side. Turn the chicken in the pan to fry all sides.

11. Place the chicken on the baking sheet with the wire rack. Bake in the oven for 25 to 30 minutes, until the internal temperature reaches 165°F. Remove and let rest for 5 minutes.

12. Make the Dijon cream sauce: Melt the butter in a small saucepan over medium heat. Add the flour and vigorously stir until the flour has completely absorbed all of the butter, about 2 minutes.

13. Add half of the milk and whisk to blend. Once smooth, add the rest of the milk and continue whisking.

14. Add the mustard, Parmesan, bouillon, and salt. Whisk well until smooth and turn off the heat.

15. Carefully remove the toothpicks from the chicken and slice into ½-inch rounds. Garnish with parsley and serve with Dijon cream sauce. Store leftovers in an airtight container in the fridge for up to 4 days. To reheat, bake at 350°F for about 10 minutes. Using the oven is recommended to get the most crunchiness.

EQUIPMENT

- **Parchment paper or plastic wrap**
- **Rolling pin**
- **Toothpicks**
- **3 medium shallow bowls, for dredging**
- **Quarter baking sheet with oven-safe wire rack**

SAM'S JOLLOF RICE WITH CHICKEN

Jollof rice is a West African staple that's made with spicy Scotch bonnet chiles, tomatoes, and an abundance of spices. If you can't find a Scotch bonnet—a small orange chile with an incredibly potent punch—it can be replaced with a habanero in a pinch. And, of course, if spice isn't your preference, reduce or omit the pepper for a milder meal. Though there are many regional versions of this dish, this recipe is inspired by Sam's home country of Nigeria.

SERVES 8

- 1½ pounds skinless, boneless chicken thighs, patted dry and cut into ½-inch cubes
- Salt and freshly ground black pepper
- 1 (14- to 15-ounce) can whole tomatoes with juices
- 1 medium red onion, quartered
- 1 red bell pepper, cored, seeded, and quartered
- 1 Scotch bonnet chile, stemmed
- ½ cup vegetable oil
- 1 medium red onion, roughly chopped
- 2 garlic cloves, minced
- 1 teaspoon minced peeled fresh ginger (optional)
- 2 tablespoons tomato paste
- 1 teaspoon dried thyme
- 2 bay leaves
- 1 tablespoon chicken bouillon paste or 1 cube chicken bouillon
- 1 tablespoon Ollie's Father-in-Law's Curry Powder (page 44) or store-bought curry powder
- 1 cup chicken broth or water
- 3 cups parboiled long-grain rice, no rinsing required (see Note)
- Chopped fresh parsley, chives, or green onion (optional)

1. Season the chicken with salt and black pepper and set aside for 10 to 15 minutes.

2. In a blender, combine the tomatoes, onion quarters, bell pepper, and Scotch bonnet chile and puree until smooth. Set aside.

3. In a large pot, heat ¼ cup of the vegetable oil over high heat.

4. Add the chicken and lightly brown, turning as needed, about 10 minutes.

Remove the chicken and set aside. Add the chopped onions and sauté them over medium-high heat until translucent, about 4 minutes. Add the garlic and ginger and sauté until fragrant, 1 to 2 minutes.

5. Add the tomato paste and cook for 2 minutes, stirring constantly so the mixture doesn't burn.

6. Stir in the tomato pepper puree, thyme, and bay leaves.

[recipe continues]

7. Cook over medium heat for 15 to 20 minutes. This mixture bubbles and splatters, so covering it loosely with aluminum foil will help keep the mess at bay.

8. Return the chicken to the pot. Stir in 1 teaspoon salt, the bouillon, curry powder, broth, and the remaining ¼ cup oil.

9. Bring to a boil and stir in the parboiled rice. Reduce the heat to low. Carefully cover the pot tightly with foil and place the lid over the foil. Cook for another 30 minutes to steam the rice, stirring after 15 minutes. While the rice is cooking, the rice on the bottom of the pan will burn slightly—this is normal and will give the jollof rice a mildly smoky flavor.

10. Stir the pot a few times before serving to incorporate the burned bits of rice with the regular rice and garnish with chopped herbs or green onion. Store leftovers in an airtight container in the fridge for up to 4 days.

NOTE: Parboiled long-grain rice is rice that has been partially cooked. Using store-bought parboiled rice helps prevent the rice from being undercooked or from getting too soggy.

EQUIPMENT
- **Stand blender**
- **Large heavy pot with tight-fitting lid or Dutch oven**
- **Aluminum foil**

JAN MAAS'S FRIED CHICKEN

While fried chicken may not be an official Christmas tradition in Holland, it's still a worthy dish to bring to a holiday potluck! This recipe results in a mouthwatering fried chicken that's crunchy on the outside and moist and juicy on the inside. Seasoned and flavorful, these fried chicken pieces are great served hot or cold.

SERVES 4

- 4 chicken drumsticks
- 4 bone-in, skin-on chicken thighs

Seasoning
- 1 tablespoon onion powder
- 1 tablespoon garlic powder
- 2 teaspoons ground ginger
- 2 bay leaves
- 1 tablespoon salt
- High-smoke-point oil, such as canola or avocado, for frying

Egg Wash
- 1½ cups buttermilk (see Note)
- 1 egg
- 2 tablespoons hot sauce
- 1 tablespoon salt
- 1 teaspoon freshly ground black pepper

Dredging Mixture
- 2 cups all-purpose flour
- 1 cup cornstarch
- 1 tablespoon salt
- 1 tablespoon celery salt
- 1 tablespoon freshly ground black pepper
- 1 tablespoon paprika
- 2 teaspoons onion powder
- 2 teaspoons garlic powder
- ½ teaspoon ground cayenne pepper
- ½ teaspoon ground ginger
- 1 teaspoon dried oregano
- 1 teaspoon dried thyme

1. To parboil the chicken, place the chicken pieces in a pot and add enough water to cover the meat.

2. Add the seasonings and bring to a boil over high heat. Once boiling, cover, reduce the heat to medium, and cook for 15 minutes.

3. Turn off the heat and let sit for at least 15 minutes. Remove the chicken and set aside.

4. Heat 1 inch of oil in the frying pan over medium-high heat.

5. While the oil is heating, prepare the dredging station. Mix together the egg wash ingredients in one large shallow bowl. In another large shallow bowl, whisk together the dry dredging ingredients.

6. Using tongs, dip a parboiled chicken piece into the egg wash, then dip into the flour mixture to evenly coat.

7. Working in batches so as not to overcrowd the pot, carefully place a few breaded chicken pieces into the hot oil and cook, turning each side after 4 to 5 minutes, until golden brown.

8. Transfer the chicken from the oil to the wire rack or prepared plate to drain. Repeat with the remaining chicken pieces. Serve hot. Store leftovers in an airtight container in the fridge for up to 4 days. To reheat, bake at 350°F for about 10 minutes. Using the oven is recommended to get the most crunchiness.

NOTE: Buttermilk can be made by mixing 1½ cups of whole milk and 1½ tablespoons of white vinegar together. Let the ingredients sit for 5 minutes, and you've got homemade buttermilk! Jan would be impressed.

EQUIPMENT
- Large deep frying pan
- Tongs
- 2 large shallow bowls, for dredging
- Wire rack or plate lined with paper towels

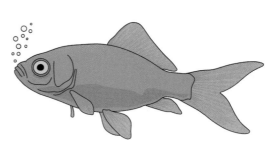

CROWN AND ANCHOR FISH AND CHIPS

Fish and chips and . . . football? This quintessentially British dish is the perfect pairing for cheering on your favorite premier league team (it also pairs well with a pint). In this recipe, the chips are cooked thrice: boiled, fried, and fried again, for an ultimate crunchy bite. For an authentic pub experience—minus Mae, Jeremy, Paul, and Baz—pair it with a side of malt vinegar and tartar sauce. While Ted would love it served up with quality press, wrapping the fish in parchment paper works well too.

SERVES 4

Chips
- 4 russet potatoes (about 2 pounds total), peeled and cut into ½-inch sticks
- 1 tablespoon white or malt vinegar
- High-smoke-point oil, such as canola or avocado, for frying
- Salt

Fried Fish
- 4 white fish fillets (about 1 pound total), such as pollock, cod, or halibut
- Salt and freshly ground black pepper
- 1 cup all-purpose flour
- ¾ cup ale or lager
- 1 tablespoon white or malt vinegar (see Notes)
- 1 ice cube (about 1 tablespoon)

Tartar Sauce
- ½ cup mayonnaise
- 1 tablespoon relish
- 1½ teaspoons fresh lemon juice
- ½ teaspoon Dijon mustard
- 1 tablespoon chopped fresh dill
- ½ teaspoon chopped capers (optional)
- ⅛ teaspoon salt

For Serving (optional)
- Lemon wedges
- Malt vinegar
- Fresh or frozen green peas, cooked in boiling water to desired doneness

MAKE THE CHIPS

1. Place the potato sticks in the 6-quart pot with at least 4 quarts of cold water. Add the vinegar and bring to a rolling boil over high heat. Boil for 5 minutes. This process removes the extra starch from the potatoes, which will make the chips super crispy.

2. Drain the potatoes in a colander and set aside for 5 minutes to let the potatoes dry out. You can help remove the excess moisture by blotting the potatoes with a paper towel.

3. Pour enough oil in the frying pan until it is about 2 inches deep and set

[recipe continues]

SEASON 1, EPISODE 5

over high heat until the oil temperature reaches 350°F.

4. Working in batches, carefully place the potatoes in the hot oil and deep-fry for 4 minutes, or until slightly cooked but not yet golden brown. Use the fine-mesh skimmer to scoop out any tiny potatoes or batter crumbs after each batch to keep the oil clean for the next batch.

5. Once all the potatoes have been fried for the first time, increase the oil temperature to 400°F.

6. Deep-fry the potatoes a second time, again working in batches, until they're crispy and golden brown, about 4 minutes per batch.

7. Transfer the chips from the oil to the wire rack or prepared plate to drain. While still hot, sprinkle them with salt.

8. Scoop out all the crumbs that are in the oil so the oil can be reused to fry the fish.

MAKE THE FISH

1. Heat the oil to 350°F.

2. Pat dry the fish with paper towels and season with salt and pepper on both sides.

3. In a medium bowl, mix together ¾ cup of the flour, the ale, vinegar, and a pinch of salt and pepper. Whisk until smooth. Add the ice cube to the batter and mix lightly. In a separate shallow dish, add the remaining ¼ cup flour.

4. Once the oil has heated, dredge a fish fillet in the plain flour, then dip into the batter mixture to coat. Working in batches, carefully place 1 or 2 battered fillets in the hot oil and fry for 3 to 4 minutes per side, until the color of the batter turns golden. Transfer the fillets to the wire rack or prepared plate to drain. Repeat with the remaining fillets.

MAKE THE TARTAR SAUCE

1. In a small bowl, mix together all the tartar sauce ingredients. Keep refrigerated until serving.

2. Serve the fried fish with chips, tartar sauce, and, if desired, any or all of the optional serving suggestions. Store leftover fish and chips in an airtight container in the fridge for up to 4 days. The tartar sauce can be stored in the fridge for up to 1 week. To reheat the leftovers, bake at 350°F for about 10 minutes. Using the oven is recommended to get the most crunchiness.

NOTES: When deep-frying the fish and chips at 350°F, the oil temperature will drop once the food is added. Keep the temperature between 285°F and 325°F while frying, but no need to stress over maintaining the higher temperature. Just be sure that the oil gets back to 350°F before frying the next batch!

The secret ingredient for getting a crispy exterior in this recipe is vinegar! Vinegar doesn't leave any discernible taste, and it keeps the fish crunchy long after the food has cooled down.

EQUIPMENT
- 6-quart pot
- Large deep frying pan
- Oil thermometer
- Fine-mesh skimmer
- Wire rack or plate lined with paper towels
- Medium shallow bowls for dredging

BALL IN A GOAL

Basic, unfussy, and hearty, Ball in a Goal is an uncomplicated yet satisfying meal. Inspired by the British classic known as Toad in a Hole, this dish consists of savory sausages baked into a high-rising Yorkshire pudding that's crisp and airy. Make it with any good-quality sausage, though British bangers are a classic choice. Serve with homemade gravy, and you'll score every time!

SERVES 4 TO 6

Ball in a Goal
- 1½ cups all-purpose flour
- 1½ cups whole milk
- 4 eggs
- 1 teaspoon ground mustard
- ½ teaspoon salt
- 2 tablespoons oil
- 4 British bangers or other good-quality sausages (about 1 pound total)
- 1 small red onion, sliced
- 4 thin bacon slices
- Chopped fresh thyme (optional)

Gravy
- 2 tablespoons unsalted butter
- 1 small red onion, thinly sliced
- Salt
- 2 tablespoons all-purpose flour
- 1½ cups beef broth
- 1 tablespoon fresh thyme or 1 teaspoon dried
- 1 teaspoon ground mustard
- 1½ teaspoons Worcestershire sauce
- Freshly ground black pepper

1. Make the ball in a goal: Set an oven rack in the middle position and preheat the oven to 425°F.

2. Whisk together the flour, milk, eggs, ground mustard, and salt. Let the batter rest at room temperature for about 30 minutes; this will help the gluten bonds develop so the Yorkshire pudding rises up nicely.

3. In the skillet, heat 1 tablespoon of the oil over medium-high heat. Cook the sausages for 5 minutes, or until sizzling and the sides start to crisp. Transfer to a plate and set aside.

4. Place the onion in the skillet and sauté over medium heat until slightly soft and browned, about 10 minutes. Transfer the onion to the same plate as the sausages.

5. Wrap the bacon slices around the cooked sausages. If your skillet is oven-safe, add the remaining 1 tablespoon oil and place the bacon-wrapped sausages in the skillet. Alternatively,

[*recipe continues*]

grease the bottom of the baking dish with the remaining oil and place the prepared sausages in the baking dish.

6. Bake for 5 minutes and then add the cooked onion around the sausages. Pour the batter over the onion and around the sausages.

7. Bake for 25 to 35 minutes, until golden brown and the batter has risen. Serve immediately, since the Yorkshire pudding collapses quickly after being removed from the oven.

8. While the pudding is baking, make the gravy: Melt the butter in a small saucepan over medium heat.

9. Add the onion, season with the salt, and sauté over medium heat until slightly soft and browned, about 10 minutes. Sprinkle in the flour and stir

constantly with the onions to make a roux, 3 to 5 minutes. No streaks of flour should be visible.

10. Slowly add the broth, whisking until smooth, 1 to 2 minutes.

11. Add the thyme, ground mustard, and Worcestershire sauce and continue cooking until the gravy is thickened. Season with salt and pepper.

12. Serve the pudding topped with the gravy.

EQUIPMENT

- **12-inch skillet**
- **9 × 13-inch baking dish (optional; if the skillet is oven-safe, the baking dish isn't necessary)**

GREEK MEATBALLS WITH TZATZIKI

Nate frequents a Greek restaurant in Tooting with his parents, but if you can't score the window table at your local Greek restaurant, then try making Greek food in the convenience of your own home. These Greek meatballs are a cinch to make, plus they're a great option for entertaining a gaggle of Shelleys, friends, or teammates! This recipe incorporates fresh herbs to amplify the flavor and grated onion to retain moisture. Serve on a large platter with a fresh parsley garnish and homemade Greek tzatziki sauce.

SERVES 4 AS A MAIN, 16 AS AN APPETIZER

Greek Meatballs

- 1 small red onion
- 1 pound ground beef or lamb
- 1 garlic clove, minced or grated
- ½ cup panko
- 1 egg
- 1 tablespoon chopped fresh mint
- 2 tablespoons chopped fresh parsley, plus more for garnish
- ½ teaspoon chopped fresh oregano
- ½ teaspoon salt
- ¼ teaspoon freshly ground black pepper
- 1 tablespoon olive oil

Greek Tzatziki Sauce

- ½ English cucumber, peeled, grated, and hand-squeezed to remove excess water
- 1 cup plain whole milk Greek yogurt
- 1 garlic clove, minced or grated
- 1½ tablespoons olive oil, plus more for drizzling
- 1½ teaspoons fresh lemon juice
- ½ teaspoon salt
- 1 tablespoon chopped fresh dill
- ¼ teaspoon freshly ground black pepper

For Serving

- Basmati rice (page 45; see Notes)
- Pita bread
- Cut-up fresh veggies, such as cucumbers and tomatoes (optional)

1. Make the Greek meatballs: Set an oven rack in the middle position, and preheat the oven to broil.

2. Coarsely grate the onion into a large bowl. Add the ground beef, garlic, panko, egg, mint, parsley, oregano, salt, and pepper and mix by hand until well combined.

3. Divide the meat mixture into 4 equal parts. Quarter each part and roll to make 4 meatballs, each with a diameter of 1¼ inches. Repeat with the remaining meat.

4. Arrange the meatballs on the prepared baking sheet. If using

[recipe continues]

skewers, spear 4 meatballs with each skewer and set the skewers on the baking sheet. Brush or drizzle olive oil onto the meatballs.

5. Broil the meatballs for 15 to 20 minutes, flipping halfway through.

6. Remove from the oven. The meatballs should be nicely browned but still juicy inside and register 160°F when an instant-read thermometer is inserted into one.

7. While the meatballs are in the oven, make the tzatziki sauce: In a small bowl, mix together all the ingredients. Chill until ready to use. Drizzle extra olive oil on top of the sauce before serving.

8. Garnish the meatballs with parsley and serve with tzatziki sauce, basmati rice, pita bread, and, if desired, fresh vegetables.

NOTES: If you have extra herbs when you're done cooking the meatballs, toss them in with the cooked rice for a fancy flourish. A squeeze of lemon is a great addition too.

Hosting a gaggle of teammates? Use this recipe to make 16 mini meatball bites. Adjust the cooking time, checking on them at the 10-minute mark.

EQUIPMENT
- **Coarse grater**
- **Parchment-lined quarter baking sheet**
- **4 metal skewers (optional)**
- **Cooking oil brush (optional)**

SEASON 2, EPISODE 5

FETTUCCINE ALFREDO

Fettuccine Alfredo is a decadent dish filled with creamy cheese and garlic-infused butter—it's no wonder Ted's addicted to this pasta. It's an impressively mouthwatering meal that's easily whipped up with maximum flavor payout. Even though it's too rich for Ted's blood, it's still a winner winner fettuccine dinner!

SERVES 4

- Salt
- 1 pound fettuccine
- ½ cup (1 stick) unsalted butter
- 1 garlic clove, minced
- 1 cup heavy cream
- 1 cup grated Parmesan
- ½ cup grated Romano
- Freshly ground black pepper (optional)
- Chopped fresh parsley (optional)

1. Pour 3 to 4 quarts of water into a large pot and add 1½ tablespoons salt. Bring to a boil over high heat and cook the pasta according to the package instructions.

2. While the pasta is cooking, melt the butter in a large saucepan over medium heat. Add the garlic and ¼ teaspoon salt and cook for 2 to 3 minutes, until fragrant.

3. Reduce the heat to low. Whisk in the heavy cream and fold in the Parmesan and Romano.

4. Remove the sauce from the heat, add the cooked pasta, and quickly stir.

5. If desired, garnish with pepper and parsley. Serve hot. The fettucine is best served immediately, but leftovers can be stored in an airtight container in the fridge for up to 4 days.

BISCUITS WITH THE BOSS

There's a whole lot of Ted Lasso magic in these biscuits—use them to win over your boss, your coworkers, or anyone else in your life who may need a sweet treat to numb the sting of defeat. Warning: Friendship may ensue! For instructions on how to re-create Ted's signature pink bakery box, see page 142.

MAKES 16 BISCUITS

- 1 tablespoon unsalted butter, at room temperature, for greasing
- 1½ cups all-purpose flour
- ½ cup almond flour
- ½ cup granulated sugar
- ½ teaspoon coarse salt
- 1 cup (2 sticks) unsalted butter, cubed and chilled
- 1 teaspoon vanilla extract or paste
- Pinch of turbinado sugar (optional)

1. Set an oven rack in the middle position and preheat the oven to 350°F. Grease the baking dish with butter and set aside.

2. Pulse both flours, the granulated sugar, and salt in the bowl of a food processor to combine.

3. Add the butter and vanilla and pulse until the dough resembles wet sand.

4. Transfer the dough into the baking dish, evenly smoothing it with an offset spatula.

5. Using your hands, firmly press the mixture into the dish to flatten the mixture. If the mixture is too sticky, lay a piece of parchment paper on top of the dough during this process.

6. Bake for 30 to 35 minutes, until the top is lightly golden.

7. Remove from the oven, sprinkle with the pinch of turbinado sugar, and let cool before cutting. Store in an airtight container at room temperature for up to 3 days, in the fridge for up to 2 weeks, or in the freezer for up to 3 months.

> **EQUIPMENT**
> - 8 × 8-inch baking dish
> - Food processor
> - Offset spatula
> - Parchment paper (optional)

TOUGH COOKIE BISCOTTI

There's a tough cookie on every team, and this tough cookie biscotti is as sweet as it is refreshing. Meyer lemon zest complements the almond and provides a lovely aromatic scent as it bakes (you can also play around with different fruit and nut combinations). This Italian-inspired biscotti is made with no butter and is baked in the oven twice—effectively removing the moisture and resulting in a cookie that is extra crunchy and, well, tough. Perfect for dunking in a cup of hot tea or milk—or for crushing your opponents on the football pitch.

MAKES ABOUT A DOZEN BISCOTTI

- Zest from 2 Meyer lemons
- 1 cup sugar
- 2 teaspoons baking powder
- ¼ teaspoon salt
- 2½ cups all-purpose flour, plus more for dusting
- ¾ cup dried blueberries
- 1 cup dry toasted slivered almonds
- 4 eggs, at room temperature
- ½ teaspoon vanilla extract
- ¼ teaspoon almond extract
- 1 teaspoon fresh lemon juice

1. Set an oven rack in the middle position and preheat the oven to 350°F.

2. In a large bowl, use your fingers to rub together the lemon zest and sugar until fragrant.

3. Add the baking powder, salt, and flour and mix.

4. Toss the blueberries and almonds into the flour mixture and set aside.

5. In a small bowl, whisk together the eggs, vanilla, almond extract, lemon juice, and 1 teaspoon water.

6. Pour the egg mixture into the flour mixture and, using your hands, combine the ingredients. Then knead to form a dough that holds together.

7. Transfer the dough to the prepared baking sheet and, using your hands, shape into a 6 × 9-inch loaf.

8. Dust the top with flour and bake for 30 minutes, or until fragrant, toasted, and the top starts to crack and expand. Transfer to a wooden cutting board to cool.

9. Use the serrated knife to cut the biscotti into slices ½ to ¾ inch thick.

10. Place the biscotti back on the baking sheet, with the flat side up.

11. Return the biscotti to the oven and bake for about 20 more minutes, flipping halfway through. The biscotti are done when the tops turn golden.

[recipe continues]

Remove and let cool before serving. Store in an airtight container lined with parchment paper (to absorb excess moisture) at room temperature for up to 4 weeks.

EQUIPMENT
- **Parchment-lined half baking sheet**
- **Large metal turner**
- **Serrated knife**

HIGGINS'S MINI CUPCAKES

Mini and charming, these white cupcakes are a perfectly dainty treat for birthdays, office parties, or other occasions where people deserve a delicious treat. Pair with American buttercream frosting and pop them into a gift box for a cute presentation. Even though these mini cupcakes were originally meant for Trent Crimm's three-year-old daughter, we know Higgins would be more than happy to share. If you don't have a mini muffin pan, this recipe works in a regular cupcake pan, but be sure to bake the larger cupcakes for 20 to 25 minutes.

MAKES ABOUT 48 MINI CUPCAKES OR 2 DOZEN REGULAR CUPCAKES

Vanilla Cupcakes
- ¼ cup (½ stick) unsalted butter, at room temperature
- ¾ cup granulated sugar
- 2 eggs, at room temperature
- ⅓ cup sour cream
- ¼ cup avocado or refined coconut oil
- 1 tablespoon vanilla extract
- 1¾ cups cake flour
- 1½ teaspoons baking powder
- ½ teaspoon baking soda
- ½ teaspoon salt
- ⅔ cup whole milk

Frosting
- ¼ cup (½ stick) unsalted butter, at room temperature
- ¼ teaspoon vanilla extract
- Pinch of salt
- 1¼ cups powdered sugar
- Sprinkles or other decorations (optional)

1. Make the mini cupcakes: Set an oven rack in the middle position and preheat the oven to 350°F.

2. In a large bowl with the electric mixer on medium-high speed, beat together the butter and sugar until light and fluffy.

3. Add the eggs, sour cream, oil, and vanilla and beat until combined.

4. Reduce the speed to low and add the flour, baking powder, baking soda, and salt. Continue mixing until combined.

5. Gradually add the milk and mix until smooth.

6. Fill the prepared mini cupcake pans with batter so each cup is about two-thirds full. A mini cupcake scoop is handy if you have one.

7. Bake for 12 to 15 minutes, until the tops are golden and a toothpick inserted in the center comes out clean.

8. Remove and cool completely before frosting.

[recipe continues]

9. Make the frosting: In a large bowl with the electric mixer on medium-high speed, beat the butter until light and fluffy.

10. Beat in 1 tablespoon water, the vanilla, and salt.

11. Reduce the speed to low and slowly beat in the powdered sugar ¼ cup at a time.

12. Once the powdered sugar is fully incorporated, gradually increase the speed to high and beat for 1 to 2 minutes, until light and fluffy.

13. Using a knife, spatula, or piping bag, spread the frosting onto the cupcakes and, if desired, decorate with sprinkles. Store in an airtight container at room temperature for up to 3 days or in the refrigerator for up to 1 week.

EQUIPMENT
- **Electric mixer**
- **2 lined mini muffin pans**
- **Mini cupcake scoop (optional)**

EARL GREY TRUFFLES

These decadent truffles are infused with Earl Grey tea, but they don't taste anything like hot brown water. Don't forget to believe in yourself when rolling them out, because truffles can be messy and don't always turn out perfectly round. Still, they are so heavenly that they are worth the effort. Enjoy these truffles just as they are, or do as Rebecca does and sandwich them between Ted's Biscuits with the Boss (page 70). It's biscuits o'clock!

MAKES 1 DOZEN TRUFFLES

- ⅓ cup heavy cream
- 2 Earl Grey tea bags
- 2 ounces dark chocolate, finely chopped
- 2 ounces milk chocolate, finely chopped
- 1 tablespoon unsalted butter, at room temperature
- Cocoa powder, for rolling

1. In a small saucepan, heat the cream with the tea bags over medium heat until simmering. Turn the heat off and steep until the cream turns latte colored, about 10 minutes.

2. Carefully remove the tea bags from the cream, squeezing them to ensure the mixture retains maximum flavor. Turn off the heat.

3. Add the chopped chocolates and butter to the saucepan, stirring quickly until incorporated. If the mixture has cooled down too much before this step, just turn the heat to low to aid in the melting process.

4. Once smooth, transfer the mixture to the fridge to firm up, about 1 hour.

5. Scoop out a small amount of ganache with a melon baller and roll into a ball using your hands. Roll each ball in the cocoa powder to finish. Let sit at room temperature for 15 minutes before serving. Store leftovers in an airtight container at room temperature for up to 3 days or in the fridge for 2 weeks.

> **EQUIPMENT**
> - Melon baller or small cupcake scoop

CHERRY TARTT

This cherry tart is sassy and full of flavor, but luckily it won't set you back £25,000 at a charity auction! A sweet cherry filling tops the shortbread, which has a touch of sass thanks to the ground ginger. Cut the tart into small pieces and enjoy while singing "Cherry Tartt doo-doo doo-doo doo-doo."

SERVES 6 TO 8

- 1 cup all-purpose flour
- ½ teaspoon salt
- ⅓ cup plus 2 tablespoons sugar
- ½ teaspoon ground ginger
- Zest from 1 lemon
- ½ cup (1 stick) plus 2 tablespoons unsalted butter, cubed and chilled

- 1 (16-ounce) bag frozen cherries, thawed
- 2 teaspoons cornstarch
- 3 tablespoons all-purpose flour
- 1 teaspoon fresh lemon juice
- ⅓ cup raw sliced almonds

1. Set an oven rack in the middle position and preheat the oven to 375°F.

2. In a medium bowl, mix together the flour, salt, ⅓ cup of the sugar, the ginger, and lemon zest.

3. Using your fingers or a pastry cutter, rub the butter into the flour until it forms pea-size clumps and resembles coarse wet sand. Transfer ½ cup of the flour mixture to a small bowl and set aside for the crumb topping.

4. Gradually add 1 tablespoon water, more if needed, and gently combine with your fingertips until the dough comes together.

5. Transfer the mixture to a tart pan and press firmly and evenly into the bottom and sides of the pan using your fingers. Dust the top of the tart with a bit of flour if the mixture sticks. Since this is a tart, don't strive for perfection—a rustic crust gets the job done!

6. Poke the dough all over with a fork and pop the crust into the oven. Bake for 10 to 12 minutes, until the edges look slightly golden. Remove from the oven and let cool completely.

7. While the tart is cooling, mix together the cherries, cornstarch, flour, the remaining 2 tablespoons sugar, and the lemon juice in a large bowl.

8. Add the sliced almonds to the reserved flour mixture and toss together.

> **EQUIPMENT**
> - Pastry cutter (optional)
> - 14 × 4½-inch rectangular pan or 9-inch round tart pan

9. Pour the filling evenly over the cooled tart. Top with the crumb topping. Reduce the heat to 350°F and bake for 30 minutes, or until the filling bubbles and the crumb topping starts to get golden.

10. Remove from the oven and let cool. Remove the tart from the pan and cut into 6 to 8 pieces. Store at room temperature for up to 12 hours or covered in the fridge for up to 3 days.

SEASON 1, EPISODE 4
SEASON 1, EPISODE 5
SEASON 2, EPISODE 6

SEXY CHRISTMAS CHOCOLATE FONDUE

Sexy Christmas parties aren't just for the holidays—you can celebrate sexy Christmas anytime, any day of the year. This whimsical platter can be made for any occasion: girls' night in, date night, movie night, or even just a rainy day. Be sure to add a variety of fresh snacks to prevent a sugar overload. This board is definitely Keeley approved!

SERVES 2 TO 4

Ideas for the platter
- **Apple slices**
- **Banana slices**
- **Biscuits with the Boss (page 70)**
- **Chopped walnuts, peanuts, or pecans**
- **Donuts**
- **Marshmallows**
- **Meringues**
- **Pineapple chunks**
- **Popcorn**
- **Pretzel rods**
- **Strawberries**
- **Stroopwafels**
- **Tough Cookie Biscotti (page 72)**

Fondue
- **5 ounces semi-sweet chocolate, chopped (about 1 cup)**
- **3 tablespoons heavy cream**
- **¼ teaspoon vanilla extract**
- **Pinch of salt**

1. Arrange whatever fruits and snacks you desire on the serving platter. Set skewers, if using, or small forks alongside the platter for dipping fruit into the fondue.

2. In a small saucepan, combine the chocolate, heavy cream, vanilla, and salt over medium heat. Bring to a light simmer, stirring constantly until the chocolate is melted and the mixture is smooth. (Alternatively, combine the ingredients in a microwave-safe bowl and heat in 20-second increments, stirring between each, until melted. Or, if you have a fondue kit, follow the manual's instructions.)

3. Transfer the fondue to a serving bowl and let cool for a minute or two. Place the bowl on the platter and enjoy immediately before the fondue hardens. Store leftovers in an airtight container in the fridge for up to 3 days. Reheat in the microwave in 20-second increments to desired consistency.

EQUIPMENT
- **Large platter**
- **Skewers (optional)**
- **Fondue set (optional)**
- **Bowls of various sizes**

SEASON 2, EPISODE 4

COACH BEARD'S CHECKMATE CHESS PIE

Coach Beard is more than just Ted's loyal right-hand man; he's also a master chess player. This classic southern dessert is a tribute to Coach Beard's brainy hobby. Enjoy it paired with a tall glass of sweet tea and a friendly game of chess. Checkmate!

SERVES 6 TO 8

- 1 sheet premade 9-inch piecrust, or frozen 9-inch pie shell, thawed
- 3 tablespoons unsalted butter
- 1 cup granulated sugar
- ½ cup pure maple syrup
- ¼ cup heavy cream

- 2 teaspoons vanilla extract
- 4 eggs, at room temperature
- 3 tablespoons cornmeal
- Whipped cream, powdered sugar, or ice cream, for topping

1. Set an oven rack in the middle position and preheat the oven to 325°F. Line a 9-inch pie plate with the piecrust and set aside.

2. In a small saucepan, brown the butter over medium-high heat until it turns slightly dark and smells nutty, 5 to 8 minutes. Remove from the heat and set aside to cool.

3. In a separate bowl, whisk together the sugar, maple syrup, heavy cream, vanilla, eggs, and cornmeal. Whisk in the cooled butter until combined.

4. Pour the mixture into the prepared pie plate. Bake for 50 minutes, or until the crust is browned and the filling is set. Allow to cool and then serve with any of the suggested toppings. Store for up to 24 hours at room temperature or covered in the fridge for up to 3 days.

EQUIPMENT
- 9-inch pie plate

KNICKERBOCKER GLORY

This over-the-top ice cream sundae is almost as good as practicing headers with your favorite uncle or reading *A Wrinkle in Time*—any pint-size football player will love it. An epic British sundae that never disappoints, the Knickerbocker Glory is extra impressive—it's no wonder that Phoebe requests ice cream for dinner. Serve it in a large sundae glass, and layer tangy compote between layers of vanilla ice cream. Don't forget to top with heaps of whipped cream and sprinkles!

MAKES 4 SUNDAES

Strawberry Compote
- **1 (16-ounce) bag frozen strawberries**
- **1 tablespoon honey**
- **1 tablespoon fresh lemon juice**

Assembly
- **Vanilla ice cream**
- **Chocolate sauce**
- **Whipped cream**
- **Sprinkles**

1. In a small pot, combine the frozen strawberries, honey, and lemon juice. Bring to a boil over medium-high heat and cook, covered, for 8 to 10 minutes.

2. Reduce the heat to medium-low, remove the lid, and cook for an additional 10 minutes at a gentle boil, or until the strawberries are thawed. Remove from the heat and, using a wooden spoon or potato masher, mash the strawberries until slightly crushed. Let cool completely and chill in the fridge. The sauce will be thin after cooking but will thicken in the fridge.

3. Assemble sundaes by alternating layers of strawberry compote and ice cream into each glass. Top with chocolate sauce, whipped cream, and sprinkles. Store leftover compote in the fridge for up to 2 weeks.

> **EQUIPMENT**
> - **Wooden spoon or potato masher**

SEASON 1, EPISODE 9
SEASON 2, EPISODE 3
SEASON 2, EPISODE 8

BELIEVE CUPCAKE SHEET CAKE

This larger-than-life cupcake sheet cake is big enough to feed a whole football team, and it works like one too. In this recipe, the individual cupcakes work together to create something amazing (sort of like AFC Richmond itself)! Keep it simple with a basic buttercream frosting and store-bought cupcake mix so you can focus on the construction. To keep the prep spaced out, make the frosting 24 hours in advance. This allows the colors to deepen, and it helps break up the tasks into more manageable steps. Before you know it, you'll have a team of twenty-four sweet treats.

MAKES ONE 24-CUPCAKE SHEET CAKE

- 24 cupcakes, any flavor, baked and cooled

Frosting Base
- 2½ cups (5 sticks) unsalted butter, at room temperature
- 2 tablespoons vanilla extract
- ¾ teaspoon salt
- 10 cups powdered sugar

Yellow Frosting
- 2 cups frosting base
- ¼ teaspoon yellow food coloring

Blue Frosting
- ½ cup frosting base
- ¼ teaspoon navy food coloring

Black Frosting
- ½ cup frosting base
- ½ teaspoon black food coloring

1. Make the frosting base (see Notes): In a large bowl with the electric mixer on high speed, beat the butter until light and fluffy, 8 to 10 minutes. Add the vanilla and salt and beat on low speed for 1 minute until incorporated.

2. Stop the mixer and add 5 cups of powdered sugar. Beat on low for 1 minute until incorporated. Stop the mixer and add the remaining 5 cups of sugar. Beat on low until incorporated. Add ¼ cup of water and raise the speed to high. Beat for 5 minutes until fluffy.

3. Divide the frosting base equally among four small bowls. Mix the yellow food coloring in the first bowl, the blue food coloring in the second, and the black food coloring in the third. The remaining frosting, in a fourth bowl, will be your white base.

4. Assemble the cake: Arrange the cupcakes in a rectangle on the cake board, 6 rows across and 4 columns down. Make sure the cupcakes are touching one another and that there is as little space as possible between cupcakes. Keep the more uniform-looking cupcakes on the edge of the rectangle and the less pretty cupcakes on the inside of the rectangle.

5. Once the cupcakes are roughly positioned in a rectangle, use a small dollop of white frosting to secure each cupcake to the bottom of the board. If some of the cupcakes are harder to work with because of their lopsided shape, then gently peel or cut the part of the cupcake that's imperfect.

6. Begin the base frosting layer with the white frosting: Spread a thick layer of white frosting over all the cupcakes. You can use an offset spatula and directly spread the frosting from the bowl to the cupcakes or you can pipe several thick lines of frosting all over the cupcakes using a #104 tip.

7. Apply this layer as evenly as possible to cover any gaps and bumps (it's okay if it's thicker in some areas that need more coverage). Once the layer of white frosting is on, let it sit for about 15 minutes to slightly crust over.

8. Apply the yellow frosting: Using a clean toothpick and a ruler, gently outline a 6½ × 11-inch rectangle on top of the white frosting. This rectangle will be the base for the yellow "BELIEVE" sign. Keep outlining the rectangle gently in the frosting until you're happy with the shape.

9. Cut a ¼-inch corner off a piping bag and fit it with the #104 tip. Fill the piping bag halfway with the yellow frosting. Practice piping the frosting on the wax paper a few times before you start decorating the cupcakes.

10. Trace the outline of the rectangle you made in step 8 in yellow frosting on top of the white frosting. Continue to fill in the shape until the entire rectangle is yellow. With a clean offset spatula, gently smooth the yellow frosting so the piping lines and the toothpick sketches aren't visible. Let this crust for about 15 minutes.

11. Use a clean toothpick to sketch the word "BELIEVE" centered in the yellow rectangle.

12. Once you're happy with the placement of the word, fill a clean piping bag halfway with the blue frosting. Cut a ¼-inch corner off the bag and fit it with the #4 piping tip. Using firm, consistent pressure, apply the blue frosting over the letters you sketched with the toothpick.

13. Fill a clean piping bag halfway with black frosting. Cut a ¼-inch corner off the bag and fit it with the #104 tip. Pipe 4 black diagonal lines in all the corners of the yellow rectangle to represent tape.

14. Transport carefully and pull apart to share! Store leftovers at room temperature for up to 3 days or in the fridge for up to a week.

[*recipe continues*]

NOTES: If your bowl isn't big enough to accommodate the full amount of butter and powdered sugar, then make the frosting base in two batches.

Gel food coloring is incredibly pigmented, which works great for achieving vibrant colors. However, this also means that less is more—so start with a small amount of coloring before adding more. Also, be sure to color your frosting at least 1 day before, as the color will gradually darken over time. Before using the frosting, give it a good stir to remove any pesky air bubbles.

EQUIPMENT

- ▦ **Electric mixer**
- ▦ **4 small bowls**
- ▦ **13 × 19-inch cake board or a half baking sheet to hold the cupcakes**
- ▦ **Offset spatulas**
- ▦ **4 frosting piping bags**
- ▦ **Piping tips (petal tip #104 and round decorating tip #4)**
- ▦ **Several toothpicks**
- ▦ **Ruler**
- ▦ **Small piece of wax paper, to practice piping**

VOLCANO CAKES FOR TWO

Sometimes opposites attract in love, as is the case with Roy and Keeley. Sometimes volcanic personalities mesh with those that are more playful and sincere. These volcano cakes are filled with chocolate lava and are dedicated to all those "tough on the outside" personalities that are soft, mushy, and lovable on the inside. This recipe serves two, perfect for sharing with your other half.

MAKES 2 (5-OUNCE) CAKES

- 3 tablespoons unsalted butter, plus more for greasing, at room temperature
- 1 teaspoon Dutch process cocoa powder, plus more for dusting
- 2 ounces bittersweet chocolate, chopped
- 1 egg, at room temperature
- 1 egg yolk, at room temperature

- ½ teaspoon vanilla extract
- Pinch of salt
- 3 tablespoons packed dark brown sugar
- 1 tablespoon plus 2 teaspoons all-purpose flour
- Whipped cream, powdered sugar, or ice cream, for topping

1. Set an oven rack in the middle position and preheat the oven to 425°F.

2. Grease the ramekins with butter and dust with cocoa powder, lightly tapping to remove the excess. Set aside.

3. In a small microwave-safe bowl, combine the butter and chocolate and heat in 15-second increments, stirring between each to combine. Let cool.

4. In a separate bowl, whisk the egg, egg yolk, vanilla, salt, and brown sugar until thick, about 3 minutes.

5. Gradually whisk the cooled chocolate mixture into the egg mixture.

6. Using a spatula, fold the flour and the 1 teaspoon cocoa powder into the chocolate mixture.

7. Evenly divide the batter between the prepared ramekins. Bake for 8 to 9 minutes, until the edges look firm but the center is slightly jiggly.

8. Remove and let cool for 1 to 2 minutes before running a knife around the edges of the ramekin. Flip the ramekin upside down on a plate and gently shake out the lava cake. Serve immediately with any of the suggested toppings. Store covered in the fridge for up to 5 days.

NOTE: What makes these volcano cakes so fun is the gooey chocolate lava center, so be diligent to not overcook this tiny cake!

EQUIPMENT
- 2 (5-ounce) ramekins

BREAD PUDDING

If you're making a list of famous British desserts, bread pudding should probably be at the top. A staple for English sweet tooths, it's a delightfully rich combination of bread and custard. Devour it for a decadent breakfast with a generous heap of whipped cream and fruit, or serve it as an after-dinner dessert with vanilla ice cream. Either way, this fantastic bread pudding is a breeze to pull together. This recipe calls for toasting fresh brioche; however, day-old crusty bread is traditionally used and works well.

SERVES 4 TO 6

- ¼ cup (½ stick) unsalted butter, plus more for greasing, at room temperature
- 1 loaf brioche, cut into 1-inch slices, lightly toasted
- ½ cup golden raisins
- 2 cups whole milk
- 1 cup heavy cream

- ⅓ cup granulated sugar
- ¼ cup packed dark brown sugar
- Pinch of salt
- 2 teaspoons vanilla extract
- 1 teaspoon ground cinnamon

- ¼ teaspoon ground cloves
- 3 eggs
- 3 egg yolks
- Whipped cream, maple syrup, and powdered sugar, for topping (optional)

1. Set an oven rack in the middle position and preheat the oven to 350°F.

2. Grease the baking dish with butter and distribute the toasted brioche slices evenly in the dish. Scatter the raisins on top.

3. In a small saucepan, heat the butter, milk, cream, sugars, salt, vanilla, cinnamon, and cloves over medium-low heat, whisking until the butter is melted, about 5 minutes. Set aside to cool. Once cool, whisk in the eggs and yolks.

4. Pour the egg and milk mixture over the bread and let sit for a few minutes so the bread has time to absorb it.

5. Bake for 30 minutes, or until the top is golden. Let cool for 10 minutes. Serve as is or topped with any of the optional suggestions. Store (without toppings) in an airtight container in the fridge for up to 5 days.

NOTE: If you're in a time crunch and need the egg mixture to cool quickly, temper the eggs by gradually adding a tablespoon of the heated milk mixture into the eggs and whisking quickly to combine. Pour the egg mixture slowly so that the eggs don't cook and clump up. Once there are equal amounts of egg mixture and heated milk mixture, pour the egg mixture back into the heated milk mixture and whisk vigorously.

> **EQUIPMENT**
> - 9 × 13-inch baking dish

STICKY TOFFEE PUDDING

Contrary to its name, sticky toffee pudding does not feature toffee. It actually gets its deep flavor from dark molasses and sweet dates. Act like the Brits do and try serving this dessert at teatime—its sweet flavors pair great with hot brown water.

SERVES 12

Sticky Toffee Pudding
- ½ cup (1 stick) unsalted butter, plus extra for greasing, at room temperature
- 8 ounces pitted dates (about 15 dates)
- 1 teaspoon baking soda
- 1 cup packed dark brown sugar
- 2 eggs, at room temperature
- 1 teaspoon vanilla extract
- 3 tablespoons molasses
- 1½ cups all-purpose flour
- 1½ teaspoons baking powder
- ¼ teaspoon salt
- ⅓ cup heavy cream

Sauce
- ¼ cup (½ stick) unsalted butter
- ½ cup packed dark brown sugar
- ½ cup heavy cream
- 2 tablespoons molasses
- Ice cream, for serving (optional)

1. Set an oven rack in the middle position and preheat the oven to 350°F. Grease the baking pan with butter and set aside.

2. In a small saucepan, bring 1½ cups water and the pitted dates to a boil over medium-high heat. Whisk in the baking soda and remove the pan from the heat. Let the dates sit for 15 minutes, or until pliable and soft.

3. Using a fork, mash the dates and water into a thick, smooth paste. Set aside.

4. In a large bowl with the electric mixer on high speed, cream together the butter and sugar until light and fluffy, about 4 minutes.

5. With the mixer speed reduced to low, add the eggs one at a time. Beat well until combined. Beat in the vanilla, molasses, and date paste. The mixture might start to look coagulated during this step, but the ingredients will mix cohesively once the flour and heavy cream are added in step 7.

6. In a separate bowl, whisk together the flour, baking powder, and salt.

7. Alternate adding the flour mixture and the heavy cream to the date mixture. Beat for 30 seconds on medium speed before adding the next increment. The final mixture will resemble cake batter.

[*recipe continues*]

8. Fill each muffin mold two-thirds full with batter.

9. Bake for 20 to 25 minutes, until the cake is set. Set aside while you make the sauce.

10. In a small saucepan, mix together all the sauce ingredients and bring to a boil over high heat. Reduce the heat to medium and soft boil for about 5 minutes without stirring, until the sauce thickens to a pourable consistency. Remove from the heat,

quickly whisk, and pour the sauce on top of the cakes. The pudding and sauce can be stored separately in the fridge for up to 5 days.

NOTE: This works in an 8 x 8-inch pan too! Just adjust the cooking time to 35 to 40 minutes, until the center is set.

EQUIPMENT
- Electric mixer
- **Jumbo muffin pan (see Note)**

STRAWBERRY ETON MESS

This British recipe might have an intimidating name, but it's hardly a mess at all. In fact, this gluten-free dessert is incredibly simple to make and can be put together with store-bought meringues. An Eton mess can be filled with any summer berry, but this recipe features a winning combination of fresh strawberries and cream.

SERVES 4

- 10 small to medium meringues (about 2 ounces total)
- 1 pound strawberries, hulled and diced
- 1 teaspoon fresh lemon juice
- 1 tablespoon strawberry preserves or other red jam

- 1 teaspoon honey
- 1¼ cups heavy cream
- 2 tablespoons powdered sugar, plus more for topping
- 1 teaspoon vanilla extract

1. Coarsely chop the meringues and set aside.

2. Toss the strawberries with the lemon juice, jam, and honey in a large bowl. Mash with a fork or potato masher until the consistency is thick and chunky (don't overdo it).

3. In a medium bowl with the electric mixer on medium speed, beat the heavy cream with the powdered sugar and vanilla until stiff peaks form, 1 to 3 minutes, taking care not to overbeat.

4. Evenly divide the chopped meringues, strawberry sauce, and whipped cream among the four glasses, alternating layers until each glass is filled.

5. If any whipped cream remains, divide it evenly among the glasses and use it as the final layer. Top with powdered sugar and serve. Store leftovers covered in the fridge for up to 3 days.

NOTE: If you're in a pinch for time, just combine the strawberry mixture, whipped cream, and meringues together in one large bowl and serve.

> **EQUIPMENT**
> - Potato masher or fork
> - Electric mixer

KEEBECCA PIE

Keebecca Pie is inspired from a popular British dessert, the banoffee pie. This pie is a magical friendship of surprising culinary pairings: a hint of cinnamon enhances the graham cracker crust, and ripe bananas are pillowed in thick dulce de leche and topped with voluminous whipped cream. Though this recipe is a pinch to whip up, making and cooling the dulce de leche can take half a day, so plan accordingly so you have ample time to make this. It might not make sense on paper, but just like Keeley and Rebecca's friendship, this pie is something special, and it's dedicated to besties everywhere.

SERVES 6 TO 8

- 1½ cups crumbled graham crackers (from about 12 graham cracker sheets)
- ¼ cup granulated sugar
- 6 tablespoons unsalted butter, melted
- ½ teaspoon ground cinnamon
- 2 (14-ounce) cans sweetened condensed milk, labels removed

- 2 cups heavy cream
- ¼ cup powdered sugar
- 1 teaspoon vanilla extract
- 2 to 4 bananas, sliced into ⅛-inch rounds
- Grated chocolate, for topping (optional)

1. Set an oven rack in the middle position and preheat the oven to 350°F.

2. In the bowl of a food processor, pulse the graham crackers, sugar, butter, and cinnamon until combined. Scrape the mixture into the pie plate, pressing down with your fingers to evenly distribute.

3. Bake for 10 minutes, or until the crust is fragrant. Remove and set aside to cool.

4. To make the dulce de leche, place the cans of condensed milk into a large stockpot of water. Cover with at least 1 inch of water and bring the water to a boil over high heat.

5. Once boiling, reduce the heat to medium so that the water slow boils. Check on the cans constantly to make sure they are always covered by water—when the water level gets low, add more water. Don't leave the pot unattended, since that could be a huge safety issue.

6. Slow boil the cans for 3½ to 4 hours. The longer the cans boil, the darker and thicker the dulce de leche will be.

7. Turn off the heat and allow the cans to cool in the water naturally before removing and opening them.

8. In a medium bowl with the electric mixer on medium speed, beat the heavy cream with the powdered sugar and vanilla until stiff peaks form, 1 to 3 minutes.

9. Pour 1½ cups of the dulce de leche into the piecrust (save the leftovers for another use) and smooth with the offset spatula. Clean the spatula after using. Layer the sliced bananas on top of the dulce de leche, pushing them down slightly into the filling. Top with whipped cream and smooth with the offset spatula. Cover loosely with aluminum foil and store in the fridge until ready to eat. If desired, sprinkle with grated chocolate before serving. The pie is best served immediately, but leftovers can be stored covered in the refrigerator for up to 3 days. Store the dulce de leche in the fridge for

up to 2 weeks and use for pie drizzle, cookies, coffee, s'mores, or eat as is!

NOTES: Alternative pressure cooker method: Place the sweetened condensed milk cans in the pressure cooker and cover with water. Pressure cook on high for 40 minutes, followed by natural release for 10 minutes. Allow to cool in the pressure cooker before using the cans.

EQUIPMENT
- **Food processor**
- **9-inch pie plate**
- **Electric mixer**
- **Offset spatula**

SEASON 1, EPISODE 2
SEASON 2, EPISODE 12

LION VS. PANDA CAKE

Keeley wants to know: Are you Team Lion or Team Panda? If you're having a hard time deciding on an animal as your alter ego, make this lion versus panda cake instead. This modified Black Forest cake is made with layers of rich chocolate cake filled with a cherry compote and a mascarpone whipped frosting. Black Dutch process cocoa powder is used for a dramatic effect, though regular Dutch process cocoa powder will also work. So what's black and white and red all over? This cake!

SERVES 8 TO 10

Cakes
- 1 cup whole milk
- 1 tablespoon white vinegar
- 1¾ cups cake flour
- 1½ cups granulated sugar
- ¾ cup black Dutch process cocoa powder
- 2 teaspoons baking soda
- 1 teaspoon baking powder
- 1 teaspoon salt
- ½ cup vegetable oil
- 2 eggs, at room temperature
- 1 tablespoon vanilla extract

Cherry Water
- 1 (16-ounce) bag frozen cherries
- ½ cup Kirsch

Cherry Simple Syrup
- ¾ cup reserved cherry water
- ½ cup granulated sugar

Cherry Filling
- ¾ cup reserved cherry water
- ½ cup granulated sugar
- 2 tablespoons cornstarch
- Reserved cherries

Chocolate Ganache
- 1 cup semi-sweet chocolate chunks
- ¼ cup plus 2 tablespoons heavy cream

Whipped Frosting
- 2 cups heavy cream
- 4 ounces mascarpone cream, at room temperature
- ¼ cup powdered sugar
- 1 teaspoon vanilla extract
- Grated chocolate, for topping
- Fresh pitted cherries, for topping

1. Make the cakes: Set an oven rack in the middle position and preheat the oven to 350°F.

2. In a large bowl, combine the milk and vinegar and set aside for 5 minutes.

3. In a separate bowl, whisk together the flour, sugar, cocoa powder, baking soda, baking powder, and salt.

4. Add the oil, eggs, and vanilla to the milk and vinegar mixture and stir vigorously to combine.

[recipe continues]

5. Slowly pour the wet mixture into the dry mixture. Whisk until all the ingredients are combined. Add 1 cup hot water and stir slowly. The batter will be runny.

6. Divide the batter equally among the three prepared cake pans. Bake for 20 to 25 minutes, until a toothpick inserted into the centers comes out clean. Set the pans on wire racks and let cool completely.

7. Make the cherry water: Place the frozen cherries in a large pot with 1⅓ cups water and simmer over medium heat for 5 to 10 minutes. Remove from the heat once the cherries are thawed and the water turns red.

8. Strain the cherries through a fine-mesh strainer over a medium bowl, capturing the liquid. Set the cherries aside. Stir the Kirsch into the liquid to complete the cherry water.

9. Make the cherry simple syrup: Bring to a boil ¾ cup of the cherry water (reserve the rest) and the granulated sugar in a small saucepan over high heat. Boil to dissolve the sugar, about 10 minutes. Remove from the heat and set aside.

10. Make the cherry filling: You should have remaining about ¾ cup reserved cherry water. If it's slightly less, add more water so it totals ¾ cup. Mix this cherry water with the granulated sugar and cornstarch in a medium saucepan over medium-high heat.

11. Add the reserved cherries and whisk every few minutes as it boils. This filling will thicken as it cooks. Once the filling is thick enough to coat the back of a spoon, remove from the heat and let cool completely.

12. Make the chocolate ganache: Melt the chocolate and cream in a small microwave-safe bowl in 20-second increments, stirring between each, until smooth. Set aside.

13. Make the whipped frosting: In a medium bowl with the electric mixer on medium speed, beat all the ingredients until stiff peaks form, 1 to 3 minutes. Set aside.

14. Assemble the cake: Remove the cakes from their pans and set on the wire racks. Make sure that the layers of each cake are flat and even. Use a serrated knife to shape the tops of the cakes if necessary.

15. Place the first cake layer on the cardboard round. If using the acetate collar, wrap it around this layer of cake (see Notes). Sprinkle a few tablespoons of the cherry simple syrup on the top of the first layer of cake and wait a few minutes for it to absorb.

16. Spoon a third of the ganache onto the first cake layer, using an offset spatula to smooth it evenly to the edge of the cake layer.

17. Spoon half of the cherry filling onto the chocolate ganache. Keep the cherry filling concentrated in the center of the cake, as the weight of the additional layers will help distribute it.

18. Spoon a third of the whipped frosting over the cherry filling, keeping the frosting concentrated in the center of the cake.

19. Take a second cake and flip it so that the flat side is up. Place this layer on top of the first layer. Sprinkle the cake with a few tablespoons of the cherry simple syrup, allowing it to absorb, and then repeat steps 16 to 18 to complete the second layer.

20. Place the last layer of cake on top. Sprinkle with a few tablespoons of the cherry simple syrup, allowing it to absorb. Spread the remaining ganache on top and the whipped frosting on top of the ganache. Top with grated chocolate and fresh cherries. Keep the cake in the fridge until serving. Store leftovers covered in the fridge for up to 3 days.

NOTES: An acetate collar can be used to keep the filling contained as the cake is stacked and decorated. To set up the collar, set up the first layer of cake on the cake board. Wrap the collar around the edge of the first layer and tape the seams closed. It will look like a top hat and act as a bib to keep the cake contained as it is being assembled. Keep the collar on the cake until right before serving.

Any extra cherry simple syrup can be stored in an airtight container in the fridge for up to 2 weeks. This syrup can also be used in Keeley's cocktail, the Big Pink French 75 (page 126)!

EQUIPMENT

- **Three 8-inch cake pans, buttered and lined with parchment rounds**
- **2 wire racks**
- **Fine-mesh strainer**
- **Electric mixer**
- **Serrated knife**
- **10-inch cardboard cake round**
- **Acetate cake collar (optional; see Notes)**
- **Offset spatula**

CLASSIC BOSS BITCH

Inspired by everyone's favorite boss bitch, Rebecca Welton, this Champagne cocktail is elegant, classic, and sophisticated. A sugar cube soaked in aromatic bitters gives it an excellent crisp quality. Serve it in a very tall and intimidating Champagne glass, drink, and feel the power. You are the boss ass bitch.

MAKES 1 DRINK

- **1 sugar cube**
- **Several dashes of aromatic bitters**

- **4 to 6 ounces Champagne or dry sparkling wine, chilled**
- **Lemon twist (optional)**

Place the sugar cube in the bottom of a Champagne glass and soak with the aromatic bitters. Top with chilled Champagne. If desired, garnish with a lemon twist.

SEASON 2, EPISODE 3
SEASON 2, EPISODE 5
SEASON 2, EPISODE 12

EARL'S GREYHOUND

An ode to Earl. This classic greyhound comes together with four simple ingredients, but it's got a unique twist thanks to the rosemary-infused simple syrup. Since the drink relies on just a few ingredients, it's best to use a good-quality grapefruit juice. This drink takes only about 30 seconds to mix up, which is shorter than Earl's screen time. A great mascot for an amazing team. Ace, furry mate!

MAKES 1 DRINK

- Ice
- **2 ounces vodka or gin**
- **4 ounces pink grapefruit juice**

- **1 teaspoon Rosemary Simple Syrup (recipe follows)**
- **Sugared Rosemary, for serving (recipe follows)**

Fill a rocks glass with ice. Add the vodka, grapefruit juice, and rosemary simple syrup and stir. Garnish with the sugared rosemary.

[recipe continues]

SEASON 2, EPISODE 1
SEASON 2, EPISODE 12

ROSEMARY SIMPLE SYRUP

MAKES ABOUT ⅓ CUP

- ¼ cup sugar
- ¼ cup water

- A few fresh rosemary sprigs

Combine the sugar and water in a small pot and bring to a boil. Add the rosemary sprigs and stir until the sugar dissolves, about 2 minutes. Remove from the heat and let the sprigs steep for an additional 30 minutes. Remove and discard the rosemary. Store the simple syrup in an airtight container in the fridge for up to 2 weeks.

SUGARED ROSEMARY

MAKES 1

- 1 rosemary sprig
- 2 tablespoons Rosemary Simple Syrup (see recipe)

- Sugar, for rolling

Dip the rosemary sprig in the rosemary syrup so that it is evenly coated. Set the sprig on a wire rack, allowing the excess syrup to drip off. Let sit to harden, about 45 minutes. Roll the sprig in the sugar.

> **EQUIPMENT**
> - Wire rack

BLOODY ROY

A complex smorgasbord of briny and smoky flavors, this drink mirrors Roy's anything-but-vanilla personality. It's a great recipe for a morning brunch after group yoga or as a cure for last night's karaoke party. If you're feeling extra spicy, add a dash of horseradish and garnish to your heart's desire. No matter what you do, don't use vanilla vodka for making this drink, and remember, "He's here, he's there, he's every f---ing where!"

MAKES 2 DRINKS

Rim salt
- 1 teaspoon celery salt
- 1 tablespoon smoked paprika
- 2 teaspoons coarse salt
- ½ teaspoon garlic powder
- ¼ teaspoon chili powder
- Lemon wedge

Bloody Roy Mix
- 8 ounces tomato juice
- 4 ounces vodka
- ½ teaspoon Worcestershire sauce
- ½ teaspoon Tabasco sauce
- ½ teaspoon horseradish (optional)
- ½ teaspoon celery salt
- ½ teaspoon ground mustard
- Juice from ½ lemon (about 1 tablespoon)
- 1 tablespoon pickle juice
- Freshly ground black pepper
- 1 cup ice cubes for mixing, plus more for serving
- Green olives on cocktail pick (optional)

1. Make the rim salt: Mix together the celery salt, paprika, coarse salt, garlic powder, and chili powder on a plate.

2. Rub the lemon wedge around the rim of a highball glass and then roll the edge of the glass in the salt to coat the rim.

3. Make the Bloody Roy mix: Place the tomato juice, vodka, Worcestershire sauce, Tabasco sauce, horseradish, celery salt, ground mustard, lemon juice, pickle juice, and pepper in a mixing glass and stir well with a bar spoon.

4. Add ice to the mixing glass and stir well to chill the drink.

5. Fill the highball glass with fresh ice and, using the cocktail strainer or bar spoon, pour the drink into the highball glass. Garnish with green olives.

EQUIPMENT
- Mixing glass or measuring cup
- Bar spoon
- Cocktail strainer (optional)
- Cocktail pick (optional)

SEASON 1, EPISODE 3
SEASON 1, EPISODE 10
SEASON 2, EPISODE 5

NUTS AND BERRIES COCKTAIL

For hardcore peanut butter addicts, this cocktail fulfills all your nutty urgings. Reminiscent of a classic peanut butter and jelly sandwich, this drink is both creamy and sweet. You can even roll the rim of the glass in creamy peanut butter and dust with grated dark chocolate for a decadent twist. Ted prefers to stick his fingers in the peanut butter jar for a midnight snack, but maybe this will become his new late-night favorite.

MAKES 1 DRINK

- **1 teaspoon creamy peanut butter, for the rim**
- **1 teaspoon finely grated dark chocolate, for the rim**
- **Ice cubes**
- **1½ ounces hazelnut liqueur, such as Frangelico**
- **1½ ounces raspberry liqueur, such as Chambord**
- **3 ounces half-and-half**

1. Place the peanut butter on a plate. Roll the edge of a rocks glass in the peanut butter to evenly coat the rim.

2. Place the grated chocolate on a clean plate and then roll the edge of the glass in the chocolate so that the chocolate sticks to the peanut butter rim.

3. Fill the glass with ice, add the Frangelico, Chambord, and half-and-half, and stir.

PHOEBE'S HOT CHOCOLATE

If you need a little pick-me-up after getting red-carded for elbowing another player, this comforting, cozy, universally loved hot chocolate is for you. Creamy and smooth, it can be dressed up with marshmallows, sprinkles, or even malted milk. Enjoyable for all ages but especially perfect for little kids, it's an essential drink for keeping hands toasty at a cold match.

MAKES 1 DRINK

- **1 cup whole milk**
- **2 tablespoons heavy cream**
- **2 tablespoons unsweetened cocoa powder**

- **2 tablespoons powdered sugar**
- **½ teaspoon vanilla paste**
- **Pinch of salt**

Combine all the ingredients in a small saucepan over medium heat, whisking. Once steaming, remove from the heat, pour into a mug, and serve.

SEASON 2, EPISODE 1

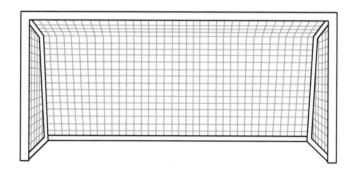

SEX ON THE PITCH

When Jamie Tartt appeared on *Lust Conquers All*, he let the world know that he was the island's top scorer, so he's probably had plenty of sex on the beach. This updated take on the classic cocktail is renamed Sex on the Pitch, so Jamie can score back where he belongs—on the football pitch. This triple-alcohol drink packs a heavy punch that even the booziest reality TV stars can appreciate.

MAKES 1 DRINK

- 1½ ounces vodka
- ½ ounce peach schnapps
- ½ ounce Chambord
- 1½ ounces orange juice
- 1½ ounces cranberry juice
- 1 teaspoon fresh lime juice
- Ice cubes

Pour the vodka, peach schnapps, Chambord, orange juice, cranberry juice, and lime juice into the shaker. Fill the shaker half to three-quarters full of ice and shake vigorously for 15 seconds. Fill a highball glass with fresh ice and strain the shaker into the glass.

EQUIPMENT
- Shaker

SEASON 2, EPISODE 1
SEASON 2, EPISODE 2

SEASON 1, EPISODE 8
SEASON 2, EPISODE 4

DANI'S CHEEKY MEXICAN PONCHE

Festive and fruity, this Mexican ponche, a traditional Mexican punch typically enjoyed during the Christmas holiday season, is perfect for large gatherings. Filled with fruits, nuts, and spices, the ingredients are easily tweaked depending on your preferences. Some of these ingredients are found only at specialty stores, but they're crucial for getting a robust and unique flavor—so you may have to put some effort into sourcing them. Feel free to add more tequila—especially since it's necessary for getting a little cheeky. Ponche is life—so make enough to give away joy for free!

SERVES 15 TO 20

- 4 quarts water
- 6 guavas, peeled and quartered
- 3 apples, cored, then cut into chunks or sliced
- 2 pears, cored, then cut into chunks
- 1 orange, sliced (unpeeled)
- 1 piloncillo cone or 1 cup packed dark brown sugar

- 2 tablespoons dried hibiscus flowers
- 10 whole cloves (about ½ teaspoon)
- 4 cinnamon sticks
- 4 star anise
- 8 pitted prunes (about ⅓ cup)
- 10 pecan halves (about ¼ cup)
- 1 cup tequila, or more to make it extra cheeky

1. In the stockpot, bring the water, fruit, piloncillo cone, hibiscus flowers, spices, prunes, and pecans to a boil over high heat.

2. Reduce the heat to medium, cover, and gently boil for at least 1 hour, stirring occasionally to ensure the piloncillo cone has completely dissolved.

3. Remove from the heat and stir in the tequila. Serve hot in mugs. Transfer leftovers to a bottle or large jar, cool, and store in the fridge for up to 5 days.

EQUIPMENT
- Large stockpot (at least 8 quarts)

FROZEN RED & BLUE MARGARITAS

What better way to show support for your favorite teams than with color-coordinating drinks? Vivid blue and red give these blended margaritas a playful pop. We are Richmond!

MAKES 8 DRINKS, 4 RED AND 4 BLUE MARGARITAS

- Coarse salt, for the rim
- Lime wedge, for the rim

Frozen Red Margaritas
- 3½ to 4 cups frozen strawberries
- 1 cup silver tequila
- ½ cup fresh lime juice (from 5 to 6 limes)
- ⅓ cup simple syrup
- ¼ cup triple sec or Cointreau
- Fresh strawberries for garnish

Frozen Blue Margaritas
- ¾ cup blue curaçao
- ½ cup silver tequila
- ¼ cup triple sec or Cointreau
- ¼ cup simple syrup
- ¼ cup fresh lime juice (from 2 to 3 limes)
- 5 cups ice, plus more as needed
- Fresh blueberries on cocktail picks

1. Pour coarse salt onto a plate. Rub the lime wedge around the rim of a margarita glass and then roll the edge of the glass in the salt to coat the rim. Repeat with the remaining seven glasses.

2. Make the red margaritas: Place the frozen strawberries in the blender and add the tequila, lime juice, simple syrup, and triple sec. Blend until smooth. Divide evenly among four margarita glasses and garnish with strawberries. Wash out the blender.

3. Make the blue margaritas: Mix the curaçao, tequila, triple sec, simple syrup, and lime juice in the blender. Add the ice and blend until slushy. If the margaritas are too watery, additional ice can be added. Divide evenly among the remaining four margarita glasses and garnish with blueberries.

EQUIPMENT
- Stand blender
- Cocktail picks

DIAMOND DOGS' HIGHBALL

The Diamond Dogs' highball is a simple drink. Serve it on the rocks while mulling over relationships, football plays, and the possibilities of life's existence. In short, fraternize, socialize, and drink. Diamond dogs adjourned!

MAKES 1 DRINK

- Ice cubes
- 1 ounce whiskey
- 3 ounces club soda or ginger ale
- Lemon twist (optional)

1. Fill a highball glass with ice and stir with a bar spoon to ensure the glass chills. Once chilled, strain out any melted water while reserving the remainder of the ice in the glass.

2. Add the whiskey and stir for 30 seconds.

3. Add more ice to the glass, filling it to the rim.

4. Top with club soda by pouring it slowly down the handle of the spoon, so the soda retains as much carbonation and as many bubbles as possible.

5. Quickly stir and, if desired, garnish with a lemon twist.

EQUIPMENT
- Bar spoon
- Strainer

SEASON 1, EPISODE 8

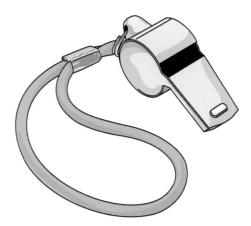

WICKEDLY FRESH MOJITO

Some *Ted Lasso* characters are favorites that we can't get enough of, like genuine football fan Tommy. He's like this drink: smooth and fresh, and we want more of whatever he's having. This classic Cuban mojito is made with rum, mint, and lime. It's incredibly zippy and refreshing, and just one sip will make you want to snap your fingers and say, "Wicked." Bonus points for scoring an ussie!

MAKES 1 DRINK

- **10 fresh mint leaves**
- **½ ounce simple syrup**
- **1 ounce fresh lime juice**
- **2 ounces white rum**
- **Ice cubes**
- **4 ounces club soda**
- **Mint sprig (optional)**
- **Lime wheel (optional)**

1. Place the mint leaves and simple syrup in a shaker. Muddle to release the mint oils.

2. Add the lime juice and rum to the shaker.

3. Fill the shaker half to three-quarters full with ice and shake lightly.

4. Fill a Collins glass with fresh ice and strain the liquid from the shaker into the prepared glass.

5. Top with club soda and, if desired, garnish with a mint sprig and lime wheel. Wicked.

> **EQUIPMENT**
> - **Shaker**
> - **Muddler**
> - **Strainer**

SEASON 1, EPISODE 1
SEASON 1, EPISODE 10
SEASON 2, EPISODE 4

BIG PINK FRENCH 75

There's no need to conquer France when you can drink it instead! Bubbly and effervescent rosé and red simple syrup lend a pink tint to the cocktail while the gin packs a subtle wallop. Add a touch of edible gold garnish for a festive and glamorous tipple.

- ⅛ teaspoon edible gold glitter, for the rim (optional)
- Lemon wedge, for the rim (optional)
- 1 ounce gin
- ½ ounce fresh lemon juice
- ½ ounce red simple syrup, such as lingonberry or grenadine syrup (see Note)
- Ice cubes
- 2 ounces sparkling rosé, chilled

1. If using, pour the edible glitter on a plate. Rub the lemon wedge around the rim of a coupe glass and then roll the edge of the glass in the glitter to coat the rim.

2. Pour the gin, lemon juice, and simple syrup into a shaker with some ice cubes.

3. Shake lightly and pour into the coupe glass. Top with rosé before enjoying.

NOTE: If you have extra syrup from the Lion vs. Panda Cake (page 103), you can use cherry simple syrup in this recipe too.

EQUIPMENT
- Shaker

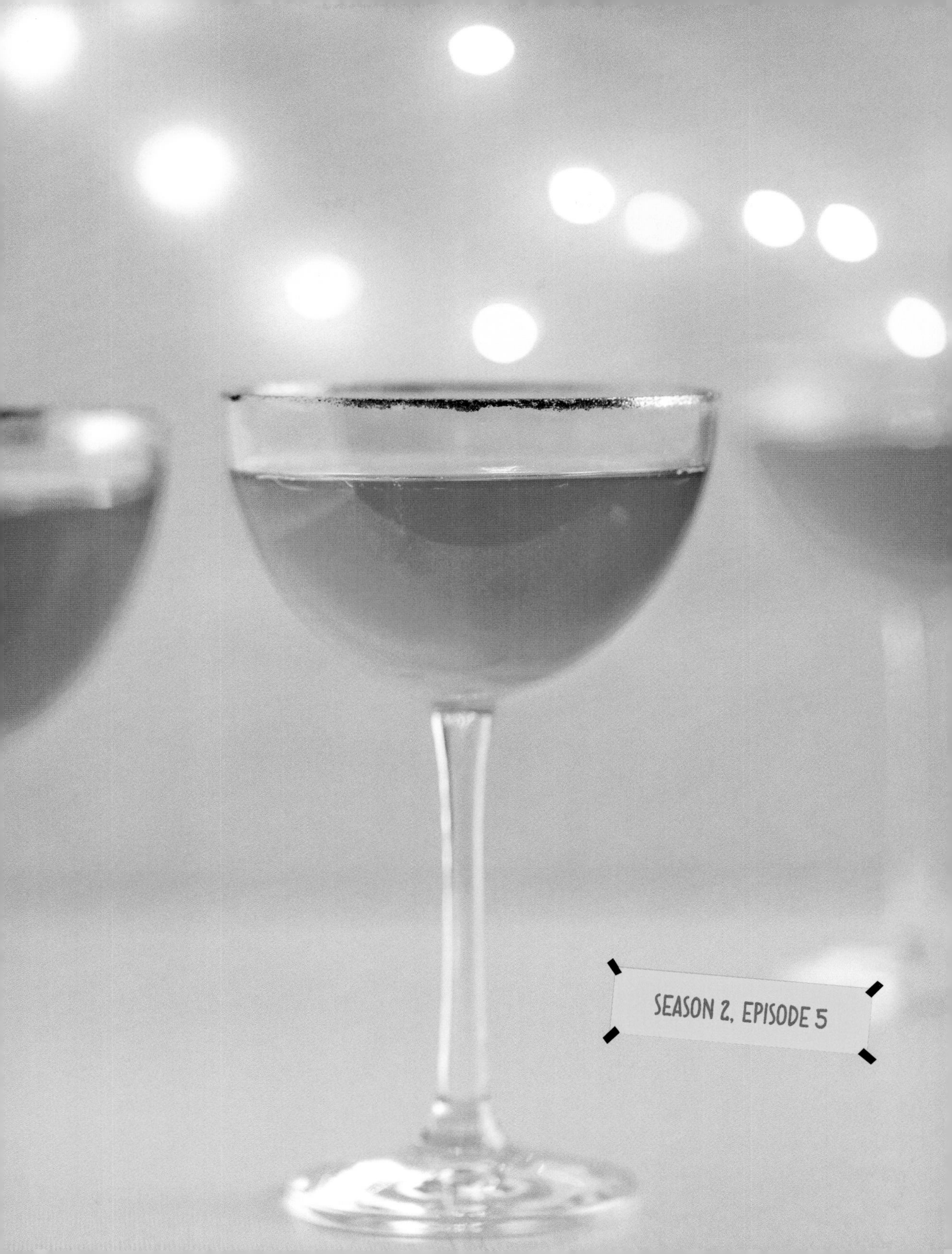
SEASON 2, EPISODE 5

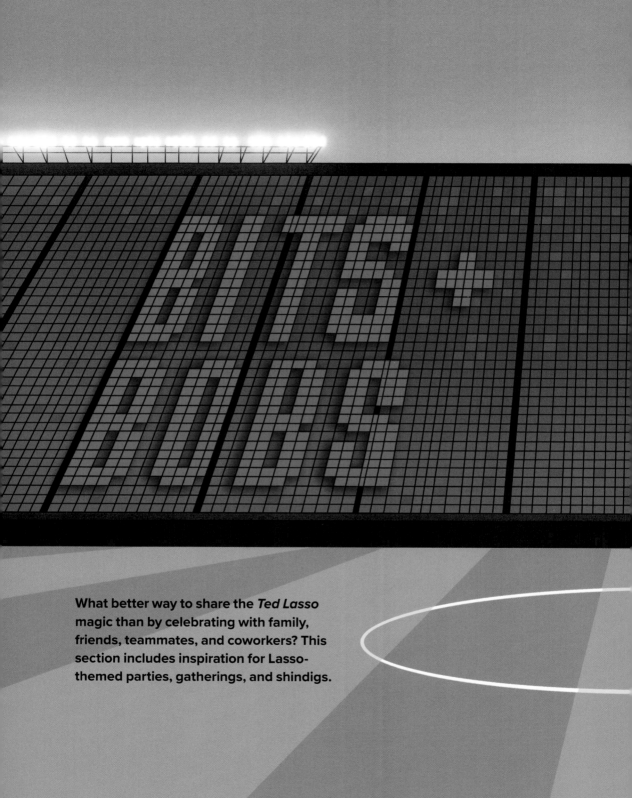

What better way to share the *Ted Lasso* magic than by celebrating with family, friends, teammates, and coworkers? This section includes inspiration for Lasso-themed parties, gatherings, and shindigs.

SEXY CHRISTMAS
AND CHARCUTERIE BOARD

Start a new holiday tradition by celebrating Sexy Christmas (although you can do this on any day that deserves a little extra sexiness). Put on your best lingerie, string up some mistletoe, grab some pasties, play a swinging Sinatra album, and set the scene with an indulgent charcuterie board. Remove the freaky orange pimentos from the olives and sip your favorite cocktails in front of a romantic fire. Remember, what happens in Richmond stays in Richmond!

Recipe Suggestions
- Chicken Cordon Bleu (page 49)
- Volcano Cakes for Two (page 93)
- Sexy Christmas Chocolate Fondue (page 82)
- Phoebe's Hot Chocolate (page 118)
- Big Pink French 75 (page 126)

Activity Ideas
- Wear pink and gold pom-pom bows.
- Light candles.
- Hang holiday stockings and mistletoe.
- Play swinging tunes.
- Light the fireplace.
- Turn on *A Christmas Story* leg lamp.

SEASON 2, EPISODE 4

INTERNATIONAL HOLIDAY PARTY

Nothing says holiday cheer quite like celebrating different meals and traditions from around the world. For this international holiday party, have guests bring their favorite foods from their own traditions to share. For this sample spread, we imagined Sam would bring Nigerian jollof rice, Dani Rojas would show up with his Mexican ponche, and the hosts might put out a few traditional British mince pies. All this food requires a large table, so feel free to improvise with a surfboard and a pool table if necessary! With this party, you can celebrate the family that you are born with, the family you make along the way, and the traditions you create with both.

Recipe Suggestions

- Richard's Fancy Stinky Cheese Board with Faux Gras (page 21)
- She's a Rainbow Fruit Board (page 10)
- Pigs in Roy's Blankie (page 15)
- Caesar You Later Salad (page 9)
- Sam's Jollof Rice with Chicken (page 51)
- Jan Maas's Fried Chicken (page 54)
- Dani's Cheeky Mexican Ponche (page 121)
- Champagne
- Mince pies
- Mulled wine

Activity Ideas

- Pop holiday crackers.
- Host a boozy secret Santa swap.
- Join caroling buskers.
- Engage in an epic Nerf gun war.
- Put on a puppet show featuring famous UK couples.
- Video call loved ones who are abroad.
- Share a little magic pixie dust.
- Attend a pagan Christmas ritual at Stonehenge.
- Spread holiday cheer by going on a secret mission while dressed in holiday attire.

GIRLS' NIGHT OUT

Get ready to embrace your inner Sassy Smurf, Stinky, and Keeley Jones with this Girls' Night Out party board. When you're ready to let loose with your besties, break out this inspirational recipe lineup for a night of decadent desserts and drinks. Liverpool karaoke bar not included.

Recipe Suggestions
- Sneaky, Salty Bitch Bites (page 4)
- Biscuits with the Boss (page 70)
- Keebecca Pie (page 100)
- Lion vs. Panda Cake (page 103)
- Earl Grey Truffles (page 78)
- Big Pink French 75 (page 126)
- Nuts and Berries Cocktail (page 117)
- Classic Boss Bitch (page 109)

Activity Ideas
- Plan a trip to Liverpool using tourist brochures and city maps.
- Go to a karaoke bar, choosing songs for your girlfriends.
- Find a cute waiter like Geoff for a single friend.
- Drink, drink, drink!

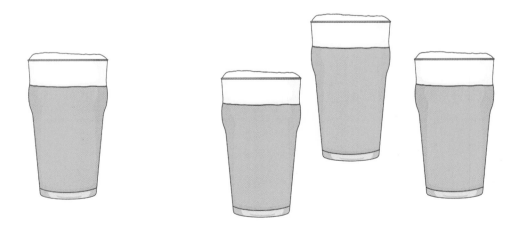

GAME-NIGHT PARTY

As the owner of the Crown and Anchor (Ted's local pub), Mae knows how to run a tight ship *and* make sure everyone has a good time. During football matches and *Gillette Soccer Saturday*s, she keeps everyone's pints, boots, and food orders fulfilled. If you'd like to run a pub out of your own home, host a game-night party and make these recipes to re-create the cozy vibe of Mae's place.

Recipe Suggestions
- Goldfish Mix (page 2)
- Southern Slaw (page 30)
- Ted's Bull's-Eye BBQ Pulled Pork Sandwich (page 34)
- Crown and Anchor Fish and Chips (page 56)
- Mum's Shepherd's Pie with Cheesy Top (page 38)
- BELIEVE Cupcake Sheet Cake (page 88)
- Frozen Red & Blue Margaritas (page 123)

Activity Ideas
- Turn on a football match (American or English!).
- Wear your favorite team jersey.
- Play snooker, darts, corn hole, billiards, or chess.
- Nurse a frothy pint.
- Contemplate the fragility of life.

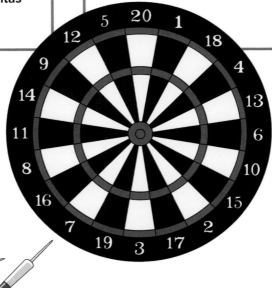

OFFICE PARTY

Ted might not know anything about English football, but his enthusiasm and kindness are contagious. Inspired by his unique ability to see the good in everyone, this office party is for all the appreciated (and underappreciated) characters that make up a team—the coach, the wonder kid, the wingman, the kitman, the powerful woman on the rise, and the boss ass bitch. This party is guaranteed to rally up some office spirit.

Recipe Suggestions

- **Sneaky, Salty Bitch Bites (page 4)**
- **Biscuits with the Boss (page 70)**
- **Earl Grey Truffles (page 78)**
- **Coach Beard's Checkmate Chess Pie (page 84)**
- **Tough Cookie Biscotti (page 72)**
- **Higgins's Mini Cupcakes (page 75)**
- **She's a Rainbow Fruit Board (page 10)**
- **Classic Boss Bitch (page 109)**
- **Diamond Dogs' Highball (page 124)**
- **Spoons of peanut butter**
- **Cups of tea or coffee**
- **BELIEVE Cupcake Sheet Cake (page 88)**

Activity Ideas

- **Hand out Ted's DIY Pink Box (page 142) filled with biscuits.**
- **Make your own BELIEVE signs.**
- **Project *Ted Lasso* reruns in the conference room.**
- **Dress up as your favorite *Ted Lasso* character.**
- **Play Sneaky, Salty Bitch Russian roulette—make a box of salty biscuits, but swap salt and sugar quantities and mix with other regular biscuit boxes.**
- **Place tiny army men around the office.**

SEASON 2, EPISODE 3

ENGLISH TEATIME

Fancy a cuppa? Host a proper English tea party with this recipe lineup. Serve classic British desserts and finger foods, and plate them on your finest China for a perfectly posh tea party. No matter where you stand on the debate of coffee versus hot brown water, this little party might just be your perfect cup of tea. So put this inspiration board together and you and your guests will be chuffed to bits!

Recipe Suggestions

- Cucumber Cream Cheese Finger Sandwiches (page 6)
- Olive Branch Savory Scones (page 17)
- Sneaky, Salty Bitch Bites (page 4)
- Biscuits with the Boss (page 70)
- Earl Grey Truffles (page 78)
- Strawberry Eton Mess (page 99)
- Cherry Tartt (page 80)
- Higgins's Mini Cupcakes (page 75)
- English breakfast, Darjeeling, Earl Grey, or your favorite British tea
- British flag shortbread
- Mini meringues
- Macarons
- Fresh fruit

Activity Ideas

- Drink tea with your pinky up.
- Have a contest to see who can fit the most little sandwiches in their mouth.
- Teapot relay race.
- Spill the tea—but no spoilers!

TED'S DIY PINK BOX

This iconic pink box is necessary if you want to truly re-create Biscuits with the Boss (page 70). Ted uses a small pink box to deliver his secret-recipe home-baked treats. We've provided a template that can be cut out and crafted so that you can make your very own pink gifting box! Bake and package several biscuits and hand them out to your favorite people. We've also included a bonus gold template so you can re-create Higgins's Mini Cupcakes container (page 75).

EQUIPMENT
- Printer
- Paper cutter or scissors
- Scoring tool or butter knife
- Glue or double-sided tape

MATERIALS
- 1 (8½ × 11-inch) piece of cardstock, ideally more than 100 lb thickness
- 1 (5 × 7-inch) piece of parchment paper, to lay inside the box

---

1. Download the PDF template from the QR code opposite.

2. Print the PDF double-sided at 100% scale (or actual size) settings so that page 1 of the PDF is on the front of the paper and page 2 is on the back.

3. Cut along the solid lines and score along the dashed lines.

4. Fold and glue the bottom front side of the box per the glue mark on the template.

5. Lay parchment paper in the box and place your treats inside!

NOTES: If there's no printer handy, any office supply store can print the box. Request that the template be printed on heavy cardstock.

Pink   Gold

Although Biscuits with the Boss (page 70) yields 16 biscuits, here's how to cut them smaller to fit 3 biscuits in 6 boxes: Slice the dish of biscuits in half vertically so there are two columns, and then slice two horizontal lines to create three rows. This will result in six rectangles.

Cut each rectangle into 3 biscuit pieces to create a total of 18 small biscuits. Each finished box will hold 3 small biscuits.

TED'S PINK BOX
(2.75 x 4.125 x 1.5 in.)

1
double sided tape
or glue

cut ——
score&fold - - - - - -

The Unofficial Ted Lasso Cookbook

ACKNOWLEDGMENTS

THANK YOU . . .

Deb Brody, Emma Effinger, Nora Gonzales, Rachel Meyers, Tai Blanche, Jennifer Eck, Beth Silfin, Robert Smigielski, and Jeanne Reina for guiding us and creating a team that embodied the Ted Lasso way: fierce encouragement, unrelenting support, and honest hard work. This book wouldn't be here if it weren't for the incredibly talented individuals at Harvest and the Gernert Company. We are truly grateful that you believed in us.

Joey and Reina and our friends for testing recipes and offering feedback and cheering us on.

Our spouses, Andy and Mas, for their love and support while we took on an extra project.

Our kids—the truest and toughest critics.

INDEX

Note: Page references in *italics* indicate photographs.

Frozen Red & Blue Margaritas, *122*, 123
Fruit. *See also specific fruits*
    Board, She's a Rainbow, 10–12, *11*
    Dani's Cheeky Mexican Ponche, *120*, 121
    Sexy Christmas Chocolate Fondue, 82, *83*

G

Gentleman's Relish Bruschetta with Burrata, 28, *29*
Gin
    Big Pink French 75, 126, *127*
    Earl's Greyhound, *110*, 111–13
Girls' Night Out, 134, *135*
Goldfish Mix, 2, *3*
Graham crackers
    Keebecca Pie, 100–101, *135*
Grapefruit juice
    Earl's Greyhound, *110*, 111–13
Greek Meatballs with Tzatziki, 63–64, *65*
Greek Tzatziki Sauce, 63–64, *65*
Greyhound, Earl's, *110*, 111–13

H

Ham and prosciutto
    Cheesy Corn, 27
    Chicken Cordon Bleu, *48*, 49–50
    Gentleman's Relish Bruschetta with Burrata, 28, *29*
    Olive Branch Savory Scones, *16*, 17
Hazelnut liqueur
    Nuts and Berries Cocktail, *116*, 117
Higgins's Mini Cupcakes, 75–77, *76*
Hot Chocolate, Phoebe's, 118, *131*
Hot Dog(s)
    Nate the Great's, Three Ways, 46–47, *47*
    Pigs in Roy's Blankie, *14*, 15

I

Ice cream
    Knickerbocker Glory, *86*, 87
International Holiday Party, *132*, 133

J

Jacket Potatoes, 24, *25*
Jan Maas's Fried Chicken, 54–55, *132*
Jollof Rice with Chicken, Sam's, 51–53, *52*

K

Kansas City Dog, 46–47, *47*
Keebecca Pie, 100–101, *135*
Knickerbocker Glory, *86*, 87

L

Lamb
    Greek Meatballs with Tzatziki, 63–64, *65*
    Mum's Shepherd's Pie with Cheesy Top, 38–40, *39*
Lemons
    Tough Cookie Biscotti, 72–74, *73*
Lettuce
    Caesar You Later Salad, *8*, 9
Limes
    Frozen Red & Blue Margaritas, *122*, 123
    Wickedly Fresh Mojito, 125
Lion vs. Panda Cake, *102*, 103–5

M

Main dishes
    Ball in a Goal, 60–62, *61*
    Chicken Cordon Bleu, *48*, 49–50
    Chicken Tikka Masala with Rice, 41–42, *43*
    Crown and Anchor Fish and Chips, 56–59, *57*
    Fettuccine Alfredo, *66*, 67
    Greek Meatballs with Tzatziki, 63–64, *65*
    Jan Maas's Fried Chicken, 54–55, *132*
    Mum's Shepherd's Pie with Cheesy Top, 38–40, *39*
    Nate the Great's Hot Dog, Three Ways, 46–47, *47*
    Sam's Jollof Rice with Chicken, 51–53, *52*
    Ted's Bull's-Eye BBQ Pulled Pork Sandwich, 34–37, *35–36*
Margaritas, Frozen Red & Blue, *122*, 123
Meatballs, Greek, with Tzatziki, 63–64, *65*
Meringue
    Strawberry Eton Mess, 99
Mexican Ponche, Dani's Cheeky, *120*, 121
Mint
    Wickedly Fresh Mojito, 125
Mum's Shepherd's Pie with Cheesy Top, 38–40, *39*

ABOUT THE AUTHORS

Aki Berry and **Meg Chano** are friends, entrepreneurs, and content creators behind the blog *Salt Harvest Creatives.* They've known each other for over twenty years, since Meg first came to America from Japan. She lived next door to Aki as a foreign exchange student, and they've been like family ever since. Food has been a huge constant in their friendship—they believe food has the power to create relationships, explore identities, and placate hangry emotions. Naturally, they're also hardcore Lasso-ists.